Are you new to computer coding but want to learn fast?

Does SQL sound like the perfect computer language for you?

This book provides clear and concise information to help you succeed!

For any newcomer to computer coding it is essential that you choose the right language to work in. while some computer languages are immensely difficult for a beginner to get their head around, there are one or two that are simple and will help you get started quicker. SQL is one of those that could see you coding in no time at all.

In this book, **Coding: Step by Step Guide, Learn Computer Coding, Take a Course to Learn SQL**, you will be led through an easy to follow process that includes chapters on:

- **What SQL is**
- **The software you will require**
- **How to create databases and tables**
- **How to input data to a database**
- **Using aggregate functions**
- **Writing SQL triggers**
- **How to make decisions with IF and case statements**
- **And more...**

You could soon be on your way to becoming adept at basic coding that will improve every aspect of your computer use, both at home and in the office. With this step-by-step guide to help you, the possibilities are limitless.

Scroll up and click Add to Cart for your copy of this amazing book now!

Coding [The Ultimate Guide]

Step by Step Guide, Learn Computer Coding, take a course to learn SQL

CONTENTS

CHAPTER ONE 6

GAME-BASED LEARNING 6

CHAPTER TWO 17

EASY TO FOLLOW GUIDANCE 17

CHAPTER THREE 23

WHAT IS SQL? 23

CHAPTER FOUR 37

WHAT SOFTWARE DO YOU NEED TO CODE SQL PROGRAMS? 37

CHAPTER FIVE 42

HOW TO CREATE DATABASES AND TABLES IN SQL? 42

CHAPTER SIX 47

WHAT ARE SQL SERVER DATA TYPES? 47

CHAPTER SEVEN 50

LEARN INPUT DATA INTO A DATABASE 50

CHAPTER EIGHT 59

HOW TO SELECT DATA FROM SQL TABLES 59

CHAPTER NINE 60

HOW TO USE AGGREGATE FUNCTIONS 60

CHAPTER TEN 63

HOW TO WRITE JOIN AND UNION STATEMENTS 63

CHAPTER ELEVEN 75

WHAT IS A SQL VIEW? 75

CHAPTER TWELVE 85

HOW TO WRITE SQL TRIGGERS 85

CHAPTER THIRTEEN 96

HOW TO WRITE STORED PROCEDURES AND FUNCTIONS 96

CHAPTER FOURTEEN 99

HOW TO MAKE DECISIONS WITH IF AND CASE STATEMENTS 99

CHAPTER FIFTEEN 105

HOW TO CONTROL THE FLOW OF PROGRAM WITH WHILE, REPEAT AND LOOP
STATEMENTS 105

CHAPTER SIXTEEN 116

WHAT ARE CURSORS AND HOW TO USE THEM? 116

CHAPTER ONE

GAME-BASED LEARNING

Game-based learning has become the most effective resolution for soft skills learning. Whereas schoolroom coaching and ancient e-learning formats are less instructive, onerous to implement, and expensive, game-based courses are the most effective thanks to training soft skills in an exceedingly fun, consistent, and cheap approach.

The combination of gamification and game-based learning is often utilized in the event of significant games, but it's vital to understand precisely what every one of those terms sits down with.

While gamification is that the use of various motivating parts like scorecards that foster competition between users, game-based learning is connected to the psychological feature space of the merchandise, its look, and its visual attractiveness.

In short, students are won over by the techniques utilized in game-based learning and captivated by the contents.

The main characteristics of game-based learning are:

- The learning method takes place through totally different and engaging eventualities
- The learning method is predicated on overcoming totally different challenges
- The learning expertise is positive and attention-grabbing

It's conjointly vital to spotlight the actual fact that to form economic game primarily based learning, and it's essential to integrate a machine that makes real things that modify students to apply the talents. Once we sit down with soft skills coaching, the utilization of video games is especially attention-grabbing. Soft skills got to be practiced so as to make sure learning.

Gamification, game-based learning, and high games pursue an equivalent goal: improve student commitment, and engagement.to make the educational expertise additional positive and enhance memory and retention.

Studies show that gamified formats of coaching in enterprises improve data retention by students, increase the completion rate of courses and create what's learned to be additionally applicable to the standard of living because of the inclusion of game parts that enable students to apply what they learn whereas learning theoretical content.

E-learning has been outlined over the past decade as the way to form out there to the scholars an oversized catalog of courses, versatile schedules, and personal coaching, however, it's established to be a system with abandonment ratios terribly high low and wherever effective learning is way below with different coaching ways.

In distinction, game-based learning offers all the benefits of securement and suppleness of e-learning coaching. However, the applying of gamification techniques improves their weaknesses. These results create it go step by step obligatory step by step within the world of on-line education and {increasingly | progressively | more and additional} can gain more land to ancient e-learning.

The catalog of game-based learning courses is presently quite little, however, make certain to finish up with an oversized a part of the web coaching sector within the future.

The game primarily based learning describes the associate degree approach to teaching, wherever students explore a relevant side of games in an exceedingly learning context designed by lecturers. Lecturers and students collaborate so as to feature depth and perspective to the expertise of enjoying the sport.

Good game-based learning applications will draw the North American nation into virtual environments that look and feel acquainted and relevant.

Within a good game-based learning setting, we have a tendency to work toward a goal, selecting actions and experiencing the implications of these actions on the approach. We have a tendency to create mistakes in an exceedingly unhazardous setting, and through experimentation, we have a tendency to actively learn and apply the proper thanks to doing things. This keeps the North American nation extremely engaged in active behaviors and thought processes that we will simply transfer from the simulated setting to the real world.

While similar, gamification could be a totally different breed of learning expertise. Gamification takes game parts (such as points, badges, leader boards, competition, actions) and applies them to a non-game setting. It's the potential to show routine, mundane tasks into refreshing, motivating experiences.

1. Measurable data

Elearning provides measurable information half-tracked in a period of time throughout every section of learning. This information may be wont to improve your learning strategy, live the impact on a business objective for quantitative ROI, and determine areas for supplementary learning, development, and training.

2. Standardize expertise

Elearning ensures the standard of your learning experiences across all sessions by reducing the variability of delivery. A facilitator's temperament, mood, material expertise, and numerous alternative factors are difficult to manage and manage in live environments.

3. customized learning

Each person is exclusive, and eLearning permits us to cater to individual learning wants. Elearning tailors learning experiences for people via self-reliant learning (allowing learners to move at their own pace). It additionally provides the flexibility to use branching eventualities, and extra supports supported user confidence levels.

4. On-demand access, out there anyplace and anytime

Access to e-learning is accessible on the work and on the go. It provides the learner period of time access to review learning on their own, once and wherever they have to. in a very live setting, the educational expertise is finite, departure the learner to accept memory or support materials.

5. Freedom to fail

Elearning provides an unintimidating and safe learning setting with low-affect assessments. It removes the concern of asking queries and reduces anxiety concerning assessments usually sweet-faced by learners in a very ancient room.

6. fast delivery cycle time

Elearning reduces roll-out time by removing several sensible limitations of ILT like trainers, location, and programming conflicts. British medium delivered e-business coaching to 23K workers in 3 months, at a value of five.9 Million pounds, compared to seventeen.8 Million and a five-year time span for room coaching.

7. cost-effective and scalable delivery

Relieve the pain of coordination, prices of materials, and problem scaling your coaching. With eLearning, you improve your ROI when it's used, whereas decreasing prices of materials, travel, and provision.

8. Optimized world providing

Ability to cost-effectively translate and localize content for various cultures supported language and regional tips and rules.

9. Enhances and supports ILT

Through a flipped model or intermingled approach, eLearning will produce uniform baseline information for all learners through pre-work or work done on a learner's own time outside in-class lessons. Elearning also can maximize time spent in ILT to specialize in follow, simulations, role-plays, and alternative live exercises.

10. Digital Medium

Since 1995 there has been a forceful increase in web users, growing from thirty-five million users to around a pair of of.8 billion users in 2015. The growing trend for digital info consumption illustrates. However, folks choose to log on for info. Elearning is the way forward for learning.

GAME-BASED LEARNING AND GAMIFICATION

Game-based learning is turning into a growing topic among 60 minutes and L&D professionals worldwide. It's been used for developing technical skills for an extended time currently, however, with the looks of game-based solutions for soft skills development, whereas game-based learning has referred to as the eye throughout the market. Within the rush, some ideas like"gamification" and"game-based learning" ar still obtaining confused.

GAMIFICATION

We can use gamification to assist our coaching functions; however, gamification isn't a coaching tool itself. Gamification uses game mechanics to interact with students in our coaching efforts. A number of the gamification techniques used are competition, stories, achievement, levels, standing, and rewards. We will definitely use these techniques to extend motivation, create our coaching fun, interact with students, and improve completion rates; however, they're going to not facilitate to form students learn. The educational method needs a plan to be learned, the flexibility to place this idea to apply, and also the risk of receiving customized feedback on visualizing the results of our performance.

HOW DOES GAMIFICATION AFFECT THE TRAINING PROCESS?

Education is any practice that constructively modifies the way we behave, think, and feel. We, as humans, always have the will to find out, no matter age. We also learn in several ways, due to intrinsic and extrinsic elements not only associated with age but also to the extent of development and maturity, personality, to experience, also as genetic and environment to permit students to use and explore their full potential, and it's a prerequisite to optimizing the tutorial methods.

How can we make education more enjoyable and more efficient? The solution lies in understanding how students learn. Basic knowledge in educational psychology is indeed what makes good instructors stand out and allows them to convey knowledge efficiently, as needed per recipient.

The main learning styles are (1) visual, counting on images and mind maps, (2) auditory, using sound, music, and rhythms, (3) physical or learning by doing,(4) verbal, using speech and writing, (5) logical, counting on reasoning to assist see the large picture, (6) social or group learning, and (7) solitary, i.e., learning alone or through self-study.

Educational methods currently used are very broad and include academic teaching, practical training, discussion, directed research, and multimedia-based learning. Technology has taken its toll on the tutorial scene like never before. Indeed, today's K-12 students are controversially called digital natives, having been born within the digital era and almost exclusively using technology in their day to day life activities. Moreover, adults and professionals also are adapting to technology and increasing their reliance thereon in their day-to-day operations, due to its omnipresence with the smartphones, tablets, computers, and, therefore, the internet. These observations suggest a robust influence of technology on all aspects of society.

In the context of education, the trend of using game elements in non-game contexts, termed otherwise gamification, aims at increasing the engagement and motivation of scholars, capturing their interest to continue learning and influencing their classroom behavior. Although games are today often utilized in educational environments, the trend remains stigmatized, and its use limited due for instance to

- inadequate access to technology,
- lack of professional expertise in integrating new technologies, and
- resistance to vary.

To change this, we'd like to know the way gamification may facilitate learning systematically.

Gamification in education may optimize the brain's processing of the latest information. This might be facilitated by the overall aspects of gamified lessons, with the audio-visual presentation, minimized bites of schematized information, short time lapses, and sometimes repetitive patterns.

New information is lost unless it's stored in our LTM through a multi-layered process involving attention, perception, selection, organization, and integration of data. The primary relay of the latest data is in our memory, which may handle only a little amount of data at a time. Miller has suggested that the human brain can process seven pieces of data at just one occasion, which can be lost in 20 seconds if not further processed to succeed in LTM.

The brain processes information within the memory using two channels—visual and auditory. When information is presented using both channels, the brain, i.e., memory, can accommodate more new information. However, information overload which can hinder the mixing of the new information into LTM. Therefore, small chunks of data got to be presented in an organized fashion. This enables the brain to integrate and organize new information to existing schemas in our LTM.

Moreover, recent research has suggested that the eye span in humans has decreased from around 12 to eight seconds. This alteration has been attributed to the digital revolution, apart from its beneficial effects, including faster response time and increased ability to multitask. These findings stress the necessity to adopt modern ways, like gamification, to transfer new knowledge and knowledge to students and teachers alike.

Gamification in education can improve motivation and engagement. Game elements like immediate feedback and earning badges for completing the challenges successfully are strongly influential on increasing the students' drive-in engaging in these games even within the walls of a classroom.

Additionally, the social component of gamified learning, whereby students gamify in groups, results in a lot of benefits on the brain function. Indeed, social, intellectual engagement activates neurotransmission within the brain, brain plasticity, and rewiring and mitigates brain inflammation and, therefore, the deleterious effects of oxidative stress on the brain. The beneficial effects of social interactions are interestingly highlighted in delaying dementia within the elderly population.

Gamification modifies the brain's reward and pleasure center and ameliorates learning. It's well established that games, whereby an individual wins or receives regeneration, can activate the brain's pleasure circuits by inducing the discharge of the neurotransmitter dopamine. Educational games are suggested to possess an equivalent influence given their elements of winning challenges or successfully achieving a goal. This pleasure during gamified education results thus during a long-lasting affinity for the tutorial subject or for solving otherwise complex problems.

Furthermore, the influence of games on the pleasure center has important effects on learning intrinsically. Indeed, reward-related signals are reported to market the storage of the latest information into LTM through dopaminergic modulation of the midbrain, which activates the hippocampus, a structure primarily involved in learning and memory. Dopamine is additionally involved in controlling neuronal plasticity within the hippocampus, which may be a significant brain phenomenon underlying the acquisition of the latest information and skills. Moreover, hippocampal memory has been reported to enhance following the practice of video games in adults through the stimulation of the brain circuits.

GAME-BASED LEARNING

That is, wherever game-based learning comes into the scene. Game-based learning happens once the sport itself is teaching the scholar. Imagine the story of a game or its characters is teaching your ideas. Suppose the sport integrates a simulation that enables students to apply those ideas and receive customized feedback. Then the educational is going on through the sport. The sport is guaranteeing experiential learning is happening. Some role-play, simulations or social psychology are samples of game-based learning utilized in the past. Computer game technology has boosted the chances of those tools. Game-learn combines each part on its coaching courses pattern and Merchants

GAME-BASED LEARNING vs. E-LEARNING COACHING

Corporate coaching has modified dramatically since the looks of on-line or e-learning merchandise. In-class space coaching has inherent disadvantages, together with being time-intense (participants need to block off giant amounts of time), onerous to coordinate, and logistically unprocurable for groups unfold across geographies. Due to these disadvantages, e-learning has become the most well-liked, cheaper various that corporations progressively embody in their coaching plans. Though e-learning courses are easier, quicker, and cheaper to implement, their quality, however, is usually poor and not comparable in-class space coaching in terms of the education delivered. Especially, the shortage of interaction and feedback, makes e-learning merchandise less effective.

Students are largely exposed to theoretical content through the shape of non-interactive slide shows or videos, that concludes with a check to gauge data acquisition. Completion rates for e-learning, not amazingly, are terribly poor and infrequently well below one-half (50%). Despite price blessings, ancient e-learning courses haven't delivered quality education or coaching. On-line game-based learning (GBL) merchandise, during this regard, deliver the most effective of each world for learning- and efficient company coaching. The game primarily based learning is partaking, academic, and motivating.

THE BENEFITS OF LEARNING THROUGH GAME

"Game" encourages youngsters to find out by making an attempt and creating mistakes, while not the concern of failure or the pressure to fulfill expectations obligatory by adults.

Integrated into an exceedingly college context, rollicking learning offers youngsters a perfect chance to place into observing and master the talents they're schooled, to be told from one another, and, above all, to guide their own learning. The results are extraordinarily positive, in step with the American Academy of Paediatrics:

- The game stimulates mental and physical health.
- The game will increase student engagement.
- Play promotes the event of govt perform.

In Finland, albeit youngsters don't seem to be at school before the age of seven, they're inspired terribly early to be told through play. From the beginning of their schooling, they're immersed {in a |during a |in an exceedingly |I n a terribly} very rollicking instructional system, and this, till higher lyceum.

The game and also the PP

The educational ideology of learning through play isn't solely well-liked within the Western world. When palmy testing, China is rolling out an outside game initiative in educational institution education referred to as Anji game across the country. In Singapore, the Ministry of Education is making an attempt to shift focus from instructional success to a brand-new vision of exploration in childhood and"targeted game."

On the IB facet, enhancements to the first Years Program (PYP) conjointly emphasize the importance of play. Lecturers give students with stimulating, engaging, and open resources to use severally, and solely act to answer children's queries and encourage them to play.

However, education professionals indicate that teaching through play also can be in the midst of many difficulties. They have to, in particular:

- Make sure to hide all learning objectives.
- Provide acceptable support to students after they have terribly inventive concepts, and it's tough to fulfill their desires.
- Set aside time to document learning within the style of visible artifacts like photos, videos, and anecdotes.
- Ensure that the total team understands learning through the game, contains a positive outlook, and is willing to alter their practices.

However, these difficulties don't forestall education professionals operating in IB world colleges from providing their students targeted, fun learning opportunities, as they justify within the following testimonies:

Vanessa writer, Confirmed Teacher - ACG college Djakarta, Indonesia

To help oldsters perceive that learning isn't restricted to lessons structured in an educational approach, we have a tendency to invited them to return and luxuriate in the study program with their youngsters, which is powerfully targeted on play and analysis. Oldsters paint and experiment with textures, count and study models, participate in construction games and participate in role-plays and writing exercises.

The game provides youngsters the chance to collaborate, develop social skills, solve issues, observe their language and digital skills, additionally as crucial thinking - all valuable life skills.

We work collaboratively with all oldsters and encourage them to attend our conferences and speak at school, additionally as participate in info sharing events, parent-teacher conferences, and interviews conducted by students.

Egypt four final

Jennifer Hernandez Stalder, PP teacher - the institution of the Taaleem network in Abu Dhabi

We have established completely different | completely different} areas within the school rooms within which youngsters will specific themselves and observe different styles of play:

- Artistic (painting, modeling made up of waste)
- Role games

Teachers conjointly take into consideration student interests so as to stimulate learning. As an example, having students regarding | inquisitive about | fascinated by} dinosaurs will offer the U.S. an excellent chance to be told additional about this animal and invite the youngsters to observe their analysis and thinking skills or to use maths ideas like size and numbers.

Teachers all interact in cooperative designing and discuss a way to teach learning objectives, skills, and ideas in AN knowledge base manner. As an example, if we have a tendency to study the activity of weight, we'll make certain to put in scales within the completely different areas of the schoolroom, like the Plasticine area, the water and sandbox area, and also the area construction. The teacher's role is to point out students a way to use weight vocabulary and to raise them inquiries to offer them challenges to figure on.

Another example is that the written expression. Our students don't have textbooks. Instead, they study the written expression in an exceedingly meaningful and targeted approach within the area dedicated to role-playing games, by writing commands or menus, or within the area dedicated to construction, by creating labels and traffic signs. Students elicit facilitate after they want it, and also, the teacher helps them observe their teaching reading and skills.

Kirsty Frost, PP teacher, and organizer - International college Ruhr, Germany

I am stunned by the thoughts and ideas of my students. I facilitate them to learn after they want it and that I encourage them to speak with one another by victimization their thinking skills to resolve issues they may encounter and answer queries that arise. Throughout the time dedicated to the sport, I take photos and shoot videos that I integrate into our digital come in order to see our learning.

If I see concepts that support our analysis module, areas of learning to deepen or qualities of the learner's profile in action, I could interrupt the course to decide a gathering. We have a tendency to then discuss our observations and that I attempt to direct the scholars towards concepts that can support the lines of analysis. It's throughout these moments that the scholars encourage ME to suppose a way to give them with the surroundings necessary to place their concepts into observe, by organizing AN excursion project, finding a specialist to ask at school or simply being careful what I want to arrange for the longer term, as an example."The game permits students to possess a say in their learning and to develop their autonomy and self-assurance. "

Teaching through games may be a long learning journey. Its effects on students' educational progress are terribly positive.

Students explore completely different musical parts, victimization multiple objects to control. I raise them inquiries to broaden their understanding, or I raise them to justify the "why" or "how" of choice to encourage them to suppose outside the box. I conjointly facilitate them to deepen this understanding by victimization completely different skills specific to learning approaches. I discovered notable variations when giving students the time and area to explore and play, including:

- A stronger commitment on their half.
- More laughter.
- An accumulated interest.

Targeted play is incredibly effective in serving to students to gift their information and passions.

At the beginning of the college year, a bunch of scholars needed to create log circuits victimization massive items of wood and spare elements. Over time, alternative students joined the journey so as to good the circuits and take a look at differing kinds of balls.

While enjoying, they place their mathematical information into observe shapes, size, weight, and numbers, and applied their social skills and their analysis and thinking skills. Additionally, the scholars experimented with the ideas of relation, balance, speed, and structure.

They have been fascinated by the development of those tracks for quite three months, and it's not finished.

As a part of our analysis module on the theme "Who we have a tendency to are," the area dedicated to role-playing in our category has become an area of exploration aimed toward responding to the growing interest of scholars for the form. They explored, adopted, and compete for the roles of receptionists, doctors, and nurses, and staged many theoretic things within which an individual might have medical facilities.

"Through role-play, students began to attach with their past experiences and use their imaginations to develop new theories that later helped them higher understand; however, the form works and the way it is often done. to repair it". "

We have noticed that after they lead the sport, youngsters develop self-assurance that keeps them intended and engaged. Moreover, their talent for asking queries, difficult common understandings, and formulating their own theories testifies to their ability to suppose creatively and critically.

The game provides youngsters authentic opportunities to observe their social skills. We've noticed that the pupils play in an exceedingly additional cooperative way: they share material and agree within the interest of their games. They conjointly show that they'll be daring and broad-minded after they favor to battle completely different roles, permitting them to expertise multiple views.

The use of role-playing in numerous contexts has reinforced students' agency, their communication skills, and also the development of a second language, deepening their imagination, empathy, understanding, and significant thinking.

Game-based learning encourages students to develop their own concepts, follow their own lines of analysis, and to work out what they need to try to. However, they need to try to to it and why to Do them.

The game conjointly has several therapeutic edges. It will facilitate students to manage a spread of feelings {and expertise | and knowledge | and skills} as they progress through the stages of their development and experience completely different things in their lives.

We have seen that learning through play contains a positive impact on our students' ability to create social bonds and manage their emotions. It conjointly helps them develop their problem-solving skills, giving them the chance to assess their successes and learn from their mistakes by making an attempt alternative solution.

CHAPTER TWO

EASY TO FOLLOW GUIDANCE

Computer coding and programming is one of the skills most in-demand in the modern world. All businesses that have an application, a website, or any hardware driven by a computer system need coders and programmers. So, if you want to become one, you have to learn to code.

With the increasing popularity of coding, the number of people trying to learn to code has increased considerably. Questions like " How to start coding " and " How to code for beginners " are fast becoming one of the main Google search queries, showing how popular it is. However, even thinking about learning to code can be difficult for a beginner.

After all, where do you start?

Well, at the end of this article, you will have a complete answer to this question. To begin, we need to ask a very important question - which many people would not be able to answer. What is coding?

What is coding?

Before you start your journey as a master programmer, you need to understand one thing: what is coding? Now, if you ask someone on the street, you may get vague answers about how computers work and how games are made.

This is not necessarily wrong, but it is really a very simplistic view of what coding is. Coding is essential in modern life because it forms the basis of everything, from computers to cars to smartphones. Without it, most modern technology would not exist as we know it, and the world would be very different.

Someone who learns to code in their spare time will likely end up using their new knowledge for one of the following:

Back-end development of the site. This is usually done in a language such as PHP or Java, and controls the functioning of a website and reacts to certain actions.

Front site development. This is done with languages such as HTML, CSS, and JavaScript, and controls the appearance of a website.

Mobile application development, which is done with something like Swift (for Apple devices) or Java.

Analysis of scientific data, which is usually done by researchers or research assistants using programs developed with Python.

These are just some of the basic works available for novice programmers. As you gain experience, you may find yourself doing more advanced things such as designing airplane autopilot systems, creating autonomous car computers, or even working with the NASA - the potential is truly endless!

Why should I learn to code?

Many new programmers who are considering coding for beginners end up doubting themselves and their ability to become a real coder. The hardest thing when trying to learn to code is to get through the first few weeks. At first, you will have trouble keeping track of what you are doing, you really will not be able to write programs, and you might even have trouble performing simple exercises or tutorials.

However, this initial doubt should be dispelled. Do your research and learn how to start coding. Follow the advice of experts and find courses that cover how to code for beginners. Some of the main reasons why you should learn coding include:

You can create your own application or website. This has the potential to open up a world of online business opportunities.

You will suddenly be much more employable. Even if the industry you work in does not need to know the code, you may find that once you have learned a new language, you are much more employable. This could lead to new job opportunities or promotions, accelerating your career.

You could start a new career. Coding is one of the most popular professions in the world. This means that there is a lot of work for good coders and that it is possible to make a lot of money as a developer or programmer.

You will learn to learn. Learning to start coding requires a lot of attention, precision, and, above all, commitment. If you can learn a programming language, it will be much easier for you to learn new skills in the future.

As you can see, you have to learn to code for many reasons. You will not only be suddenly more employable and have better job security, but you will also learn a new skill and be able to start your own online business if you wish.

What are some popular languages to learn first?

There are literally hundreds of different programming languages. Many of them have very specific use cases and are quite difficult to learn, making them unsuitable for beginners who want to learn to code for the first time.

However, there are a few very popular languages that are easy to learn, widespread, and have a large number of use cases. These languages generally have a fairly simple syntax, large online communities and are often read the same way as in English. In our opinion, some of the best programming languages to learn include:

JavaScript

JavaScript is arguably the most popular and widely used programming language. Although it is not the simplest programming language, its versatility, and the demand for programmers who master it perfectly make it an excellent language for people who want to learn to code. Some of the main reasons why JavaScript is at the top of our list of the best languages to learn in the first place include:

- It is very widespread:
  JavaScript is everywhere. It has traditionally been used for front-end website development, but it has become more popular with back-end developers in recent years. Almost everyone with a website or app will have at least JavaScript code that needs to be maintained or updated from time to time, so there will always be work for developers.
- It has greatly improved recently:
  As more and more people search for answers to questions like "How to start coding" and "How to code for beginners," the JavaScript community has grown rapidly. As more and more people start using the language, the number of tools available to developers is also increasing rapidly, which means there are many different things for which you can use JavaScript.
- The demand for developers is enormous:
  As we noted earlier, JavaScript is everywhere. Despite the recent increase in the number of people learning the language, the demand for experienced JavaScript programmers remains considerable. This means there are lots of jobs available, allowing you to choose when and where you work.
- It is not that difficult to learn:
  Of course, it is not the simplest language, but it is far from the most difficult. Once you understand the syntax and how programming works, JavaScript is a great language for beginners. If you think you can try it, go to

BitDegree. Here you will find two excellent JavaScript courses to choose from. The first, the JavaScript video tutorial, will give you an introduction to the language and how to use it. The interactive JavaScript tutorial goes into more detail and will give you a wider range of skills and more knowledge at the end of the course.

Python

Python is arguably the best language to code for beginners. It is the most popular language taught in schools around the world, probably due to its versatility and simplicity. Python grew extremely fast in 2017, placing it at the same level as JavaScript in terms of popularity. This suggests that this language will remain relevant - and therefore, useful to learn - for years to come.

Some of the strengths that make Python a great tool for those who want to learn coding include:

It is fairly simple and easy to follow, which makes it good for beginners with little or no coding knowledge.

It reads like in English, which makes the syntax easy to learn and debug.

It is extremely versatile and allows you to transfer your knowledge in areas such as web development, application building, and even analysis of scientific data.

Python is the preferred language of academics and others working in the sciences. It is used to write basic data analysis or tracking programs, which means that learning the basics of Python could be a great idea if you are a researcher.

It is also widely used in new areas such as artificial intelligence and machine learning, two of the fastest-growing industries in the past two or three years. If you are interested in new technologies and the rise of artificial intelligence, you must learn to code, and Python is a great language to learn first.

BitDegree offers four different Python courses. The first two, Knowing the basics of Python language and their new Ultimate Python training course, will teach you the basics of the language and its syntax. The next two, Learn to Create Python Data Structures and Python Image Recognition, will teach you some of the practical applications of the language and how to use it in the real world.

HTML

HTML is probably the easiest language to learn from coding languages, and it is a good option for people who are not technology-savvy but still want to learn to code. Although simple, HTML is widely used in content management and front-end web design. With CSS, it's essential for anyone looking to get a job as a front-end developer, so why not learn it first?

Even if you never intend to get into serious programming or coding, HTML can still be very useful. For example, if you regularly write code for your own website or blog, you may want to customize the content of your content. This is usually quite difficult without at least some HTML knowledge, so you should definitely try to learn it. Other times you could use HTML include:

If you need to customize an email template, HTML is used for most emails. If you know at least basic HTML, you can customize any email template you use for your business.

To create internal links. An understanding of HTML code and how it works will allow you to create internal links in your content. This is especially useful when writing long songs with lots of subcategories.

To personalize your content. Understanding HTML will allow you to change fonts, control the location of images, and control the font size when publishing new content.

As you can see, HTML is a great language for people who want to learn to code, but who may lack self-confidence. If that appeals to you, head over to BitDegree and check out their HTML 5 tutorial and their   Space Doggo HTML and CSS course, these two courses will introduce you to the language and teach you the main concepts, giving you enough information to decide if you want to learn to code.

Java

The last language on our list, Java, is one of the most popular programming languages in the world. It is used for a whole range of different things, from back-end web development to software engineering, and is popular among people who want to learn to code for beginners.

Originally designed as a simpler alternative to C ++, Java has taken off and has become extremely widespread in the world of computing and programming. The majority of large companies use Java to build their desktop applications and websites. Java is cross-platform compatible via the Java Virtual Machine (JVM), which reads and executes Java code. The majority of Android applications are also created using Java.

As you can see, Java use cases are very common. This strengthens its position as an ideal language to start learning to code. It is a high-level language, which means that it has a relatively simple syntax and conventions. It is designed for beginners who have not done a lot of programming, that is to say, that it is robust and that it can sometimes execute code even if there are small errors.

The main disadvantage of Java is that it takes a lot of code to create something worthwhile. This makes it less rewarding for people who are just starting to code. However, it is scalable, fast, and in demand.

If Java seems like a good place to start learning to code, go to BitDegree, and take a look at the courses on offer. If you are a beginner, the interactive Java tutorial is a great place to start. It will teach you how to code with Java, what Java can do, and the basics of programming.

What steps should I take to learn how to code?

It can be difficult and confusing to learn to code, especially if you don't have a lot of technological experience. Before you start your journey as a featured programmer, there are a few things you need to take to make the learning experience easier and more fulfilling, including:

Start by understanding why you want to code

If you don't already know why you want to start coding, now is the time to think about it. The reasons you want to learn to code largely determine the languages you learn, the time you spend learning, and the type of course you take. Ask yourself the following questions:

- What do you want out of coding?
- Do you want to become a career coder?
- How determined are you to learn a new programming language?

The answers to these questions should help you get started in codification.

Once you know why you are coding, choose a language

Again, you need to know why you want to learn to code before you can choose a language to learn. The right language for you and your needs will depend exactly on what you hope to gain from the learning experience.

For example, if you want to become an iOS programmer, you should probably learn Swift. If you want to work in web development, one of the languages described above will be a good choice, while Solidity is essential if you want to become a blockchain engineer.

Start simple and don't expect the world

Programming is like any other skill. Don't expect to step in directly and learn how to build your own apps or websites in a matter of hours. Unfortunately, it takes more time to develop the skills necessary to become an even decent programmer.

Once you've identified why you want to learn to code and what you hope to get out of it, choose your language, and start learning!

Resources for learning to code

Just because you sign up for an online course or tutorial doesn't mean you can't use other resources to further your learning. There are thousands of different resources in the form of websites, discussion boards, applications, and tutorials. Some of the most popular resources for programming language learners include:

- Simple programming applications. With the development of programming, an increasing number of programming applications are available to help you

learn. Although many of them are aimed at children, they can still be a very effective way to familiarize yourself with difficult concepts.
- Use free online training websites. Websites like BitDegree offer a variety of free and paid training courses that are designed to help you learn a new programming language. And the best part? If you do not have the necessary funds for a course, you can apply for a scholarship on programming for online courses.
- Take books. Sure, you might think that we are in the digital age and that textbooks are simply no longer needed, but the reality is that they are still extremely relevant. If you really want to learn to code, grab a book or three that describe the basics of the language you are learning.

These are just some of the alternative resources available for learning how to code. A quick Google search will reveal much more. Make sure you take the opportunity to get the most out of your programming course!

It's time to start learning to code

Learning coding and computer programming are becoming two very popular pastimes among young people around the world. While coding is gaining popularity, many people still find the first steps difficult, as learning a new language can be daunting at first.

If you're having trouble choosing a language to learn and getting started, be sure to read the entire article above. Start with simple, popular language like Python, Java, JavaScript, or HTML, take your time and remember: learning programming is not something you can do overnight. It takes time, effort, and, most of all, a lot of commitment.

CHAPTER THREE

WHAT IS SQL?

SQL is (Structured command language) that could be a machine language for storing, manipulating, and retrieving knowledge keep during an electronic database.

SQL is that the commonplace language for electronic database Systems. All the electronic database Management Systems (RDMS) like MySQL, MS Access, Oracle, Sybase, Informix, Postgres, and SQL Server use SQL as their commonplace information language.

Today, Structured command language is that the commonplace suggests that of manipulating and querying knowledge in relative databases, though' with proprietary extensions among the product. The benefit and omnipresence of SQL have even LED the creators of the many"NoSQL" or non-relational knowledge stores, like Hadoop, to adopt subsets of SQL or return up with their own SQL-like question languages.

But SQLwasn't continuously the"universal" language for relative databases. From the start (circa 1980), SQL had sure struck against it. Several researchers and developers at the time, together with American state, thought that the overhead of SQL would keep it from ever being sensible during production information.

Clearly, we have a tendency to were wrong. However, several still believe that, for all of SQL's ease and accessibility, the value exacted in runtime performance is commonly too high.

SQL history

In 1970, EF CODD, the research director of the IBM center in San José, invented the relational model based on relational algebra. This model is causing a revolution in the approach to databases.

In 1977, the creation of the SEQUEL language (Structured English Query Language) and implementation of the R System prototype database based on the theory of CODD. SEQUEL continues to enrich itself to become SQL (Structured Query Language).

In 1981, ORACLE CORP launched the first version of its relational database management system (RDBMS), IBM released SQL / DS, and RTI launched INGRES.

In 1982, IBM released SQL / DS for its VM / CMS environment, and the ANSI (American National Standard Institute) launched a project to standardize a relational language.

In 1983, IBM launched DB2 for the VMS environment.

In 1986, the company SYBASE launched its RDBMS designed according to the Client-Server model.

The first SQL standard (SQL-1) from ISO (International Standard Organization) appears. There are now dozens of products offering the SQL language and running on machines ranging from microphones to large systems.

Since then, the various flagship products have evolved, the SQL standard has passed to SQL-2, then SQL-3. SQL is now an essential language for any modern DBMS. On the other hand, although a standard exists, we are witnessing a proliferation of dialects specific to each product: either subsets of the standard (some functionalities not being implemented) or supersets (addition of certain functionalities, specific to each product).

Oracle and Informix dominate the current market, SQL-Server (from Microsoft) is trying to establish itself in the world of PCs under NT. Besides these very expensive products, there are fortunately free and free systems: MySQL and PostgreSQL are the best known.

Although these RDBMS do not have the power of commercial products, some are approaching them more and more. The notable differences mainly concern the development environments, which are real software workshops under Oracle and which are reduced to programming interfaces C, Python, Perl under PostgreSQL. The same goes for user interfaces: there are for PostgreSQL, but they certainly don't have the power of their commercial counterparts.

Before there was SQL, databases had tight, steering programming interfaces, and usually were designed around a network schema known as the CODASYL knowledge model. CODASYL (Committee on knowledge Systems Languages) was an association that was chargeable for the programming language (starting in 1959) and information language extensions (starting ten years later).

When you programmed against a CODASYL information, you were navigating to records through sets, that specific one-to-many relationship. Older ranked databases solely permit a record to belong to at least one set. Network databases permit a record to belong to multiple sets.

Say you wished to list the scholars registered in metallic element one zero one. Initial, you'd notice "CS 101" within the Courses set by name, set that because the owner or parent of the Enrolees set, notice the primary member (ffm) of the Enrolees set, that could be a Student record, and list it. Then you'd move into a loop: notice next member (ffm) and list it. Once fnm was unsuccessful, you'd exit the loop.

That may seem to be heaps of disagreeable chore for the information coder. However, it had been terribly economical at execution time. Specialists like Michael Stonebreaker of the University of CA at Berkeley and Ingres observed that doing that kind of question during a CODASYL information like IDMS took roughly [*fr1] the hardware time and fewer than [*fr1] the memory because of the same question on an electronic database exploitation SQL.

Relational databases and SQL

Why would you surrender an element of 2 improvements in swiftness and memory use? There have been two huge reasons: easy development and movability. I didn't assume either one mattered abundant in 1980 compared to performance and memory necessities, however as constituent improved and have become cheaper, individuals stopped caring concerning swiftness and memory and distressed a lot of concerning the value of the development.

In different words, Moore's Law killed CODASYL databases in favor of relative databases. Because it happened, the advance in development time was important, however SQL movability clad to be a fantasy.

Where did the relative model and SQL return from? E.F."Te" Codd was a computer user at the IBM San Jose workplace WHO found out the speculation of the relative model within the Sixties and printed it in 1970. IBM was slow to implement a {relational information| electronic database |on-line database |computer database | electronic information service} in a trial to guard the revenues of its CODASYL database IMS/DB.

Once IBM finally started its System R project, the event team (Don Chamberlin and Ray Boyce)wasn't below Codd, and that they unnoticedCodd's 1971 Alpha relative language paper to style their own language, SEQUEL (Structured English question Language). In 1979, before IBM had even discharged its product, Larry writer incorporated the language in his Oracle information (using IBM's pre-launch SEQUEL publications as his spec). SEQUEL before long became SQL to avoid a global trademark violation.

The"tom-toms beating for SQ" (as Michael Stonebraker place it) were coming back not solely from Oracle and IBM, however conjointly from customers. It wasn't simple to rent or train CODASYL information designers and programmers. Therefore SEQUEL (and SQL) looked way more enticing. SQL was, therefore, enticing within the later Eighties that a lot of information vendors basically fastened a SQL question processor on prime of their CODASYL databases, to the good dismay of Codd, WHO felt that relative databases had to be designed from scratch to be relative.

A pure electronic database, as designed by Codd, is made on tuples classified into relations, per first-order predicate logic. Real-world relative databases have tables that contain fields, constraints, and triggers, and tables area unit connected through foreign keys. SQL is employed to declare the information to became, and a SQL question processor and question optimizer flip the SQL declaration into a question set up that's dead by the information engine.

SQL includes a sub-language for outlining schemas, the information definition language (DDL), at the side of a sub-language for modifying knowledge, the information manipulation language (DML). Each of those has roots in early CODASYL specifications. The third sub-language in SQL declares queries, through the choose statement and relative joins.

SQL statements are grouped into categories according to their usefulness, and the entities handled. We can distinguish five categories, which allow:

- the definition of the elements of a database (tables, columns, keys, index, constraints, etc.),
- data manipulation (insertion, deletion, modification, extraction, etc.),
- management of data access rights (acquisition and revocation of rights),
- transaction management,
- and finally, the integrated SQL.

The language data definition (DDL or Data Definition Language, or DDL in English) is an oriented language at the structure of the database. The LDD allows you to create, modify, and delete objects. It also allows you to define the data domain (number, character string, date, Boolean, etc.) and to add value constraints on the data. Finally, it allows you to authorize or prohibit access to data and to activate or deactivate auditing for a given user.

The LDD instructions are: CREATE, ALTER, DROP, AUDIT, NOAUDIT, ANALYZE, RENAME, TRUNCATE.

The data manipulation language (DML, or Data Manipulation Language, or DML English) is the set of commands for manipulating data in a database. The LMD allows adding, deleting, and modifying rows, viewing the content of tables, and locking them.

The LMD instructions are INSERT, UPDATE, DELETE, SELECT, EXPLAIN, PLAN, LOCK TABLE.

These elements must be validated by a transaction for them to be taken into account.

The access protection language (or Data Control Language, or DCL in English) takes care of managing access rights to tables.

The instructions of the DCL are: GRANT, REVOKE.

The transaction control language (or Transaction Control Language, or TCL in English) manages the modifications made by the LMD, which is to say, the characteristics of the transactions and the validation and cancellation of the modifications.

The TCL instructions are: COMMIT, SAVEPOINT, ROLLBACK, SET TRANSACTION

The integrated SQL (Embedded SQL) allows the use of SQL in a third-generation language (C, Java, Cobol, etc.):

declaration of objects or instructions;

execution of instructions;

management of variables and cursors;

error handling.

The instructions for the integrated SQL are DECLARE, TYPE, DESCRIBE, VAR, CONNECT, PREPARE, EXECUTE, OPEN, FETCH, CLOSE, WHENEVER.

Traditional relational database management systems (RDBMS) offer a data model composed of a collection of relationships containing attributes each of a specific type. Commercial systems manage, for example, decimals, integers, strings, currencies, and dates. It is commonly accepted that this model is unsuitable for the data processing applications of the future because, if the relational model has successfully replaced the previous models partly thanks to its "spartan simplicity," the latter, however, complicates the implementation of certain applications. PostgreSQL provides substantial additional power by incorporating the following four basic concepts so that users can easily extend the system: classes, inheritance, types, functions. Other features increase power and flexibility: constraints, triggers, rules, transaction integrity.

These features place PostgreSQL in the category of relational-object databases. Do not confuse this category with that of object servers that do not tolerate traditional RDBMS access languages as well. So, although PostgreSQL has some object-oriented functionality, it belongs primarily to the RDBMS world. This is essentially the RDBMS aspect of PostgreSQL that we will cover in this course.

One of the main qualities of PostgreSQL is that it is free software, that is to say, free and whose sources are available. It is possible to install it on Unix / Linux and Win32 systems.

PostgreSQL works according to a client/server architecture, and it is thus constituted:

a server part, that is to say, an application running on the machine hosting the database (the database server) capable of processing client requests; in the case of PostgreSQL, a memory-resident program called postmaster;

a client part (psql) to be installed on all machines requiring access to the database server (a client can possibly run on the server itself).

Clients (the machines where the PostgreSQL client is installed) can query the database server using SQL queries.

Consider the following minimalist relational scheme:

- Actor (Num-Act, Last Name, First Name)
- Play (Num-Act, Num-Film)
- Film (Num-Film, Title, Year)

Any comparison of attributes is only accepted if these attributes are defined in the same domain. The DBMS must, therefore, constantly check the validity of the values of an attribute. This is why the command to create tables must specify, in addition to the name, the type of each column.

For example, for the Film table, it will be specified that the Title is a character string and the Year a date. When inserting tuples in this table, the system will ensure that the different fields of the tuplet satisfy the domain integrity constraints of the attributes specified when the database was created. If the constraints are not satisfied, the tuple is simply not inserted into the table.

When inserting tuples in a table (i.e., a relation), it happens that an attribute is unknown or undefined. One then introduces a conventional value noted NULL and called null value.

However, a primary key cannot have a null value. Likewise, a primary key must always be unique in a table. This strong constraint on the primary key is called relationship integrity constraint.

Any relational DBMS must check the uniqueness and the defined character (NOT NULL of the values of the primary key.

In any relational schema, there are two types of relationships:

relationships that represent entities of the modeled universe; they are called static, or independent; the Actor and Film relationships are examples;

relations whose existence of tuples depends on the values of attributes located in other relations; these are dynamic or dependent relationships; the Play relationship is an example.

When inserting a tuple in the Play relation, the DBMS must verify that the Num-Act and Num-Film values correspond, respectively, to a value of Num-Act existing in the Actor relation and a value Num-Film existing in the Film relationship.

When deleting a tuple in the Actor relationship, the DBMS must check that no tuple in the Playing relationship refers, via the Num-Act attribute, to the tuple that we are looking to delete. If necessary, i.e., if one or more corresponding Num-Act values exist in Play, four possibilities are possible:

- prohibit deletion;
- also, delete the relevant tuples in Play;
- warn the user of an inconsistency;
- set the values of the attributes concerned to a null value in the Play table, if the operation is possible (which is not the case if these values occur in a primary key);

A table is a collection of rows and columns. The creation consists of defining (according to the analysis) the name of these columns, their format (type), the default value when creating the line (DEFAULT), and the business rules applying to the column (CONSTRAINT).

The simplest command to create tables will include only the name and type of each column in the table. At creation, the table will be empty, but a certain space will be allocated to it. The syntax is as follows:

Please select

CREATE TABLE nom_table (nom_col1 TYPE1, nom_col2 TYPE2, ...)

When you create a table, you must define the integrity constraints that the data that you will put in the table must respect

The SELECT command alone is the language for querying a database. She allows to:

select certain columns of a table (projection);

select certain rows of a table according to their content (selection);

combine information from several tables (join, union, intersection, difference, and division);

combine these different operations together.

A query (i.e., a query) is a combination of operations on tables (relationships) and the result of which is itself a table whose existence is ephemeral (the time of the query).

Simplified syntax of the SELECT command

A request generally takes the form:

Please select

SELECT [ALL | DISTINCT] {* | attribute [, ...] }

   FROM nom_table [, ...]

   [WHERE condition]

the SELECT clause allows you to specify the attributes that you want to appear in the result of the query; the star character (*) retrieves all the attributes of the table generated by the FROM clause of the query;

the FROM clause specifies the tables to which the query relates;

the WHERE clause, which is optional, sets out a condition that the selected tuples must meet.

For example, to display all the tuples of the movie table, you can use the query:

Please select

SELECT * FROM film

In summary, we can say that the SELECT clause is used to perform the projection, the FROM clause the Cartesian product and the WHERE clause the selection

 Delimiters: single and double quotes

To literally specify a character string, it must be surrounded by apostrophes (i.e., single quotes). For example, to select police films, we use the query:

Please select

SELECT * FROM film WHERE genre='Policer.'

The dates must also be surrounded by apostrophes (e.g., '01 / 01/2005 ').

As the apostrophe is used to delimit strings, to represent it in a string, it must be split (example: 'the tree'), or precede it with a backslash (example: 'l \' tree').

When the name of an element of a database (a table or column name, for example) is identical to a SQL keyword, it should be surrounded by double-quotes. For example, if the purchase table has a date attribute, we could write:

Please select

SELECT "date" FROM a chat

Of course, SQL reserved words are not recommended for naming such objects. Double quotation marks are also necessary when the name (of a column or a table) is made up of particular characters such as blanks or others, which is obviously not recommended.

Translation of operators of relational algebra (part 1)

Translation of the projection operator

The projection operator Π (A 1, ... An) (relation) is simply translated into SQL by the query:

Please select

SELECT DISTINCT A_1, ..., A_n FROM relation

DISTINCT allows one to retain only one occurrence of the tuple in the case where a request produces several identical tuples.

Translation of the selection operator

The selection operator σ (pr ed predicate) (relationship) results simply by SQL query:

Please select

SELECT * FROM relation WHERE predicate

In a simplified way, a predicate is a logical expression on comparisons.

Translation of the Cartesian product operator

The Cartesian product operator relation 1 × relation 2 is translated into SQL by the query:

Please select

SELECT * FROM relation_1, relation_2

We will return to the Cartesian product in the sections

Translation of theequijoin's operator

The equijoin Ture operator relation 1 ▷ ◁ A 1, A 2 relation 2 is translated in SQL by the query:

Please select

SELECT * FROM relation_1, relation_2 WHERE relation_1. A_1 = relation_2. A_2

We will come back to the different types of joins in the section

. The general syntax of the SELECT command

Here is the general syntax for a SELECT command:

Please select

SELECT [ALL | DISTINCT] {* | expression [AS nom_affiché] } [, ...]

   FROM nom_table [[AS] alias] [, ...]

   [WHERE predicate]

   [GROUP BY expression [, ...]]

   [HAVING condition [, ...]]

   [{UNION | INTERSECT | EXCEPT [ALL]} requite]

   [ORDER BY expression [ASC | DESC] [, ...]]

In fact, the SQL SELECT order is made up of 7 clauses, 5 of which are optional:

SELECT:

This clause allows you to specify the attributes that you want to appear in the result of the query

FROM:

This clause specifies the tables to which the query relates

WHERE:

This clause allows you to filter the tuples by imposing a condition to be fulfilled so that they are present in the result of the query

GROUP BY:

This clause makes it possible to define groups

HAVING:

This clause allows you to specify a filter (condition for grouping tuples) relating to the results

UNION, INTERSECT, and EXCEPT:

This clause allows you to perform set operations between several query results (i.e., between several SELECT)

ORDER BY:

This clause makes it possible to sort the tuples of the result

SQL choose statement

The choose statement tells the question optimizer what knowledge to come, what tables to appear in, what relations to follow, and what order to impose on the same knowledge. The question optimizer should puzzle out by itself what indexes to use to avoid brute force table scans and sensible} good question performance unless the actual information supports index hints.

Part of the art of electronic database-style hangs on the considered use of indexes. If you omit the associate index for a frequent question, the full information will curtail below significant browse masses. If you have got too several indexes, the full information will curtail below significant write and update masses.

Another vital part is selecting an honest, distinctive primary key for each table. You do not solely need to take into account the impact of the first key on common queries. However, it'll play in joins once it seems like a remote key in another table, and the way it'll have an effect on the data's vicinity of reference.

In the advanced case of information tables that area unit go {different ways | get a divorce |separate |split} into different volumes betting on the worth of the first key, known as horizontal shading, you furthermore may need to take into account however the first key can have an effect on the sharding. Hint: you would like the table distributed equally across volumes, which suggests that you just don't wish to use date stamps or consecutive integers as primary keys.

SQL keep procedures

Sometimes the declarative nature of the choice statement doesn't get you wherever you would like to travel. Most databases have a facility known as keep procedures; sadly, this can be a district wherever nearly all of the databases use proprietary extensions to the ANSI/ISO SQL standards.

In SQL Server, the initial idiom for keep procedures (or keep procs) was Transact-SQL, aka T-SQL; in Oracle, it had been PL-SQL. Each database has further languages for keep procedures, such as C#, Java, and R. a straightforward T-SQL keep procedure would possibly solely be a parameterized version of a get statement. Its benefits area unit easy use and potency. Keep procedures area unit optimized once the area unit saved, not when they're dead.

A lot of sophisticated T-SQL keep procedure would possibly use multiple SQL statements, input and output parameters, native variables, BEGIN...END blocks, IF...THEN...ELSE conditions, cursors (the row-by-row process of a set), expressions, temporary tables, and an entire host of different procedural syntax. Clearly, if the keep procedure language is C#, Java, or R, you're about to use the functions and syntax of these procedural languages. In different words, despite the actual fact that the motivation for SQL was to use standardized declarative queries, within the world, you see several database-specific procedural server programming.

That doesn't quite take U.S.A. back to the dangerous recent days of CODASYL information programming (although cursors return close). However, it will walk back from the concepts that SQL statements ought to be standardized, which performance issues ought to be left to the information question optimizer. In the end, a doubling of performance is commonly an excessive amount of to go away on the table.

SQL could be a language to control information; it includes database creation, deletion, winning rows, modifying rows, etc. SQL has associated with ANSI (American National Standards Institute) commonplace language, however, their area unit many various versions of the SQL language.

The Best thanks to Learn SQL

First, you wish to grasp the fundamentals. Here are a number of steps you'll be able to want jumpstart learning SQL on your own.

1. begin easy

No matter what methodology you utilize to be told SQL, you will be concerned to quickly dive in and check your new skillset. However, take some time and concentrate on learning easy queries 1st. Don't go too complicated question writing till you are perfect the fundamentals.

2. Watch TutorialsMicrosoft's free SQL information Fundamentals tutorial provides an associate in-depth introduction to information nomenclature, skills, and ideas. SQLZOO and Codecademy additionally provide interactive tutorials that permit you to manipulate information and build queries to check your SQL data.

3. Take a SQL category

While you'll be able to teach yourself some basic SQL commands, most of the people realize that taking a SQL category is useful for effort new skills. Learning basic SQL ideas through active coaching can best prepare you for advanced SQL topics and prepare you for certification testing.

Here are some SQL categories to urge you started:

- Introduction to SQL Databases
- Querying information with interact SQL

- Developing SQL Databases
- Analyzing information with SQL Server news Services
- Oracle information – Introduction to SQL

4. Install a Free SQL information

The best thanks to learning SQL is by active it. Install free open supply information; thus, you'll be able to begin writing and running easy queries victimization your own information. MySQL could be widespread free information that's compatible with most operating systems.

Once you've learned the basics of SQL and feel snug running queries, it's time to urge certified.

Benefits of a SQL Certification

Once you have well-learned SQL, you'll take the ensuing step. If you wish to face resolute employers or move up at intervals a corporation, you'll copy your SQL data with expert certification.

SQL Server certifications are a key mortal for candidates seeking roles in info development, administration, or analysis.

Certifications not solely demonstrate your depth and breadth of technical data, however, additionally, show that you're committed to your career. Technical certifications will boost your wage up to 10% over the national average.

How to Get SQL Certified

SQL Server could be a favorite among developers. As a result, it's a lot of sturdy and easier to use than alternative info systems on the market. Like most relative databases, Microsoft SQL Server uses SQL to manage knowledgebases and question data.

Earning the MCSA: SQL Server certification proofs that you have got the essential skills required to develop and maintain vital Microsoft SQL Server environments. This certification qualifies you for a grip as an info developer or info analyst.

New Horizons offers comprehensive coaching courses to arrange for you for the MCSA SQL Server certification examination. The certification track includes three courses and exams:

Querying Microsoft SQL Server®: during this course, you'll learn the way to write down basics Transact-SQL queries meant for Microsoft SQL 2014.

Administering Microsoft® SQL Server® Databases: This 5-day course teaches you concerning the SQL Server 2014 product options and tools associated with maintaining info.

Implementing an information Warehouse together with Microsoft® SQL Server®: The last course teaches you ways to form an information warehouse, implement ETL, and validate and cleanse knowledge with SQL Server.

Once you complete these three courses and pass the corresponding tests, you're able to take the MCSA SQL Server certification examination.

Receiving your MCSA SQL Server certification can assist you in acquiring essential skills required to develop, run, and maintain ensuing iterations of advanced info and data solutions.

What Is SQL Used For?

Databases (and so SQL) are utilized in the technology field in nearly every space wherever important amounts of knowledge are concerned. Let's check up on a number of the industries that the majority usually use SQL.

In the finance business, banking applications and payment processors like Stripe store and operate knowledge regarding monetary transactions and users. Behind these processes could be sophisticated information. Moreover, bank information systems have additional security needs that decision for the best levels of risk compliance within the SQL code used.

Music applications like Spotify and mythical being additionally create intensive-use databases. Among alternative things, databases facilitate these apps to store Brobdingnagian libraries of music files and albums by numerous artists, operate this knowledge to seek out what the user is trying to find, store the info regarding users and their preferences, etc.

Social media platforms involve loads of knowledge processes. Applications like Instagram and Snapchat use SQL to store a user's profile info like bio and placement, to update the app's information once a user creates a replacement post or shares a photograph, and to record messages sent from one user to a different that the user will retrieve the messages to scan once more at a later time.

CHAPTER FOUR

WHAT SOFTWARE DO YOU NEED TO CODE SQL PROGRAMS?

The six best information software packages

Let's begin at the beginning: information may be a system that stores your info and content. That involves your customers' products, catalogs, and repositories. It's capable of making and modifying access to the info hold on there.

With an information software package, understanding and victimization info becomes easier. It allows the organization of knowledge and, therefore, the linking of knowledge between them, whereas providing reports on their changes and trends. Your information then helps you manage your selling and sales methods.

To allow you to make associate degree orderly and economical information, we provide you the highest five of the simplest software packages on the market!

1. MySQL

True reference, MySQL is out and away from the foremost fashionable information software package information for internet applications. Though it's free, it's often updated with new options and security enhancements.

For industrial use, take the paid version of MySQL that offers even a lot of functions. The sole drawback, the software system is quicker and a lot of strength than the paid version.

Easy-to-use interface and batch commands permit you to method large amounts of knowledge

MySQL additionally offers a large variety of user interfaces, and its worth is kind of cheap. It simply integrates with an alternative information software package.

2. PostgreSQL

It is the "ancestor" of the information software package. PostgreSQL may be a real passkey, compatible with platforms like Linux, and might be hosted on virtual, physical, and additionally cloud environments.

Although it may be tough to tack, PostgreSQL comes with predefined functions, which will include method terabytes of knowledge in a very simplified manner.

Another vital point: its latest version has seen a rise within the variety of users, as a result of the protection half has been greatly improved because of an in-depth word profile.

3. SAP HANA

If you would like to extract information hold on in your applications, SAP HANA is your most suitable option.

Even if he's the "new kid" of information software package, he already has nice capacities. It will method SAP and non-SAP information and facilitates information backup.

With this tool, you'll recover information from applications and alternative sources, whether or not physical or within the cloud. It combines BDD practicality, however, additionally advanced analytics, enterprise info management choices, and a well-supplied application server.

Advantages of SAP HANA software package embrace compression that reduces resource necessities, the flexibility to manage inventory, and manufacture reports in real-time. All of those functions area unit performed in RAM, among one platform.

4. Mongo DB

Mongo dB is on the market in free and paid versions. This software package will use structured and unstructured information. Note that it's adaptable, flexible, fast, straightforward, and easy to use, even for beginners. Additionally, it offers a full set of subtle pilots.

Unlike alternative information software package, it's capable of operating in non-relational variable processing things. Mongolian monetary unit dB offers impermanent search functions and simply integrates NoSQL documents.

5. Microsoft SQL Server

A classic within the world of information software package, Microsoft SQL Server, it works on each native and cloud-based server. Besides, it may be designed on each form of servers at the same time.

Available on Linux and Windows, its support for time information is one of the simplest options for its latest update. This builds it easier to stay track of the info changes you may need to make.

Another attention-grabbing feature: Microsoft SQL Server offers dynamic information protection, with single access for approved persons to sensitive information

Microsoft SQL Server: what's it?

SQL Server, usually pronounced 'Sequel Server,' isn't dangerous |a nasty |a foul} sequel to associate degree already bad motion picture. Off from it: it's an awfully powerful system that will be utilized in organizations of variable sizes, from little businesses to major firms.

SQL Server is Microsoft's electronic database management system. The key operational word here is the system; the systems operate to manage multiple databases. It additionally provides a set of tools that facilitate to create, change, and manage the information. In addition, there square measure tools for report writing, knowledge import/export, and knowledge analysis tools.

History

Sybase and Microsoft discharged version one.0 in 1989. The partnership between the two corporations fell apart within the early 90s, however Microsoft unbroken the rights to the name SQL Server. ulterior versions embody SQL Server 2000, 2005, 2008, 2012, 2014, and 2016.

SQL Server merchandise

There square measure many totally different flavors of SQL Server, which provide totally different options betting on user desires. These merchandises additionally referred to as Editions include:

- Enterprise: designed for giant organizations with difficult knowledge desires
- Standard: helpful for departments among organizations
- Workgroup: Includes a reportage module for synchronizing knowledge remotely
- Developer: Single-use installation, made for development and testing of applications
- Web: for little businesses trying to create net applications
- Express: A free edition meant for learning and education
- Compact: Another free possibility for complete applications
- Evaluation: A trial version that's solely valid for a brief fundamental quantity.

Microsoft SQL Server in Action

Like most management systems, SQL Server supports customary Structured search language (SQL). However, the system contains T-SQL (Transact-SQL).

Although SQL Server will run on a portable computer, it's normally found on a server in larger organizations. It will support thousands of users.

As its name implies, Microsoft SQL Server runs on a centralized server that permits for coinciding user access. An associate degree example of a server is an associate degree worker portal that homes information articles, personal knowledge, and self-service tasks. At any purpose throughout the day, thousands of workers may be accessing content; 100 a lot of may change personal information, and a dozen a lot of maybe accessing dashboard reports.

6. Oracle database

what is oracle database- worker entity

Each worker might have one or a lot of contacts, and you'll be able to produce a contact entity and relate the worker entity to the contacts entity through a relationship referred to as one-to-many.

WHAT IS ORACLE DATABASE - RELATIONSHIP?

By the way, we regularly refer the entities as tables, records as rows, and fields as columns.

The relative model is healthier than the file model as a result of it removes duplicate knowledge, e.g., if you place workers and make contact with info on a similar file. The worker, United Nations agency, has quite one contact, can seem in multiple rows.

The computer database Management System, or RDBMS in brief, manages relative knowledge. Oracle info is associate degree RDBMS with the biggest market share.

oracle tutorial

Besides the Oracle info, there are alternative RDBMS merchandise offered. Here are some notable ones:

- Db2 from IBM.
- SQL Server from Microsoft.
- MySQL – the foremost widespread ASCII text file info, conjointly from Oracle.
- PostgreSQL – the foremost advanced open supply info.
- Oracle database options

Oracle info permits you to quickly and safely store and retrieve knowledge. Here are the combination edges of the Oracle Database:

- Oracle database is cross-platform. It will run on numerous hardware across operating systems as well as Windows Server, Unix, and numerous distributions of GNU/Linux.
- Oracle database has its networking stack that permits application from a distinct platform to speak with the Oracle info swimmingly. For instance, applications running on Windows will hook up with the Oracle info running on the operating system.
- ACID-compliant – Oracle is ACID-compliant info that helps maintain knowledge integrity and responsibility.
- Commitment to open technologies – Oracle is one amongst the primary info that supported GNU/Linux within the late Nineties before GNU/Linux become a commerce product. It's been supporting this open platform since then.

Oracle database has many structural options that build it popular:

- Logical arrangement – Oracle uses the logical arrangement to store knowledge in order that you'll be able to act with {the knowledge |the info |the information} base while not knowing wherever the data is held on physically.
- Partitioning – may be a superior feature that permits you to divide an oversized table into totally different items and store every bit across storage devices.
- Memory caching – the memory caching design permits you to rescale really giant info that also will perform at high speed.
- Data lexicon may be a set of internal tables and views that support administer Oracle knowledgebase a lot of effectively.
- Backup and recovery – make sure the integrity of the info just in case of system failure. Oracle includes a robust tool referred to as Recovery Manager (RMAN) – permits DBA to perform cold, hot, and progressive info backups and point-in-time recoveries.
- Clustering – Oracle Real Application Clusters (RAC) – Oracle allows high convenience that allows the system is up and running while not an interruption of services just in case one or a lot of servers in an exceeding cluster fails.

Oracle Database Editions

Oracle provides three main editions of Oracle Databases as follows:

1) Enterprise Edition (EE) is the common and costly edition of the Oracle info. it's the subsequent characteristics:

- No most range of CPUs
- No limits on memory or info size
- Include premium options that aren't offered in alternative editions.

2) customary Edition (SE) may be an edition of the Enterprise Edition that has the subsequent characteristics:

- Limited to four or fewer CPUs
- No limit on memory or info size
- Include several options, however no as several as engineering

3) Expression Edition (XE) may be a free-to-use version of the Oracle info that offered on each Windows and GNU/Linux platform. These are the options of Oracle info Xe 18c:

Limited to a pair of CPUs

It can use the most of 2GB of RAM and has 12GB of user knowledge.

Very restricted options

CHAPTER FIVE

HOW TO CREATE DATABASES AND TABLES IN SQL?

Create a Database

Before You start

Limitations and Restrictions

Most of 32,767 databases will be specified on AN instance of SQL Server.

Prerequisites

The produce information statement should run in AN auto-commit mode (the default dealings management mode) and isn't allowed in an exact or implicit dealing.

Recommendations

The master information ought to be saved whenever user information is made, modified, or dropped.

When your product information, create the information files as giant as attainable, supported the utmost quantity of knowledge you expect within the information.

Security

Permissions

Requires to produce information permission within the master information, or needs to produce ANY information or ALTER ANY information permission.

To maintain management over disk use on AN instance of SQL Server, permission to make databases is often restricted to some login accounts.

Using SQL Server Management Studio

To create information

In Object somebody, connect with AN instance of the SQL Server information Engine and so expand that instance.

Right-click Databases, and so click New information.

In New information, enter an information name.

To create the information by accepting all default values, click OK; otherwise, continue with the subsequent no obligatory steps.

To change the owner's name, click (...) to pick out another owner.

Note

The Use full-text assortment possibility is often checked and dims as a result of, starting in SQL Server 2008, all user databases are full-text enabled.

To change the default values of the first knowledge and dealings log files, within the information files grid, click the acceptable cell and enter the new worth. For a lot of data, see Add knowledge or Log Files to information.

To change the collation of the information, choose the choices page, and so choose a collation from the list.

To change the recovery model, choose the choices page, and choose a recovery model from the list.

To change information choices, choose the choices page, and so modify the information choices. For an outline of every possibility, see ALTER information SET choices (Transact-SQL).

To add a brand new filegroup, click the Filegroups page. Click Add and so enter the values for the filegroup.

To add AN extended property to the information, choose the Extended Properties page.

In the Name column, enter a reputation for the extended property.

In the worth column, enter the extended property text. For instance, enter one or a lot of statements that describe the information.

To create the information, click OK.

- **Using Transact-SQL**

To create information

Connect to the information Engine.

From the quality bar, click New question.

Copy and paste the subsequent example into the question window and click on Execute. This instance creates information Sales. As a result of the keyword, PRIMARY isn't used, the primary file (Sales_dat) becomes the first file. As a result of neither MB nor K is laid out in the dimensions parameter for the Sales_dat file, it uses MB and is allotted in megabytes. The Sales_log file is allotted in megabytes as a result of the MB suffix is expressly explicit within the SIZE parameter.

SQL

Copy

```
USE master;

GO

CREATE DATABASE Sales

ON

(NAME = Sales_dat,

    FILENAME = 'C:\Program Files\Microsoft SQL
Server\MSSQL13.MSSQLSERVER\MSSQL\DATA\saledat.mdf',

    SIZE = 10,

    MAXSIZE = 50,

    FILEGROWTH = 5)

LOG ON

(NAME = Sales_log,

    FILENAME = 'C:\Program Files\Microsoft SQL
Server\MSSQL13.MSSQLSERVER\MSSQL\DATA\salelog.ldf',

    SIZE = 5MB,

    MAXSIZE = 25MB,

    FILEGROWTH = 5MB);

GO
```

SQL create Table statement

In information theory, a table may be a structure ("basic unit") accustomed to store knowledge within the information.

I love to use analogies plenty. Therefore I'll jazz here too. If you think that of a library, information is one shelf with books, and every book may be a table. Every book has its own contents however is somehow associated with alternative books on the identical shelf – either by sharing some properties, either by simply being shut.

There is plenty of theory behind information tables, and the way to make a decision what goes wherever, however the only you'll do is following. After we check up on our knowledge and that we got to decide what goes wherever we should always cluster knowledge in tables in such a way that everything that belongs to identical real-life entities goes to an identical table.

E.g., if we wish to store knowledge describing cities and countries, we'll have two separate tables in our information – one for cities and another one for countries. We tend to won't combine their knowledge, however rather relate them. This goes out of the scope of this text and shall be coated within the future elements of this series.

To outline a table, we'll follow the syntax. You'll see full T-SQL produce Table syntax here. However, I'll over again modify the statement:

CREATE TABLE table_name (

   Column_name column_type,

   column_name column_type,

   ...

);

We will simply choose the name for our table and list all the columns we want in this table. Columns are also called attributes, and every column describes a property of one record in the table. The column has its type, and we should choose the type based on values we expect in that column (number, text, etc.).

SQL Create Table example

Let's take a look at the definition of our two tables:

First, we'll define the city table.

-- Table: city

CREATE TABLE city (

   id int NOT NULL IDENTITY(1, 1),

   city_name char(128) NOT NULL,

   lat decimal(9,6) NOT NULL,

   long decimal(9,6) NOT NULL,

   country_id int NOT NULL,

```
        CONSTRAINT city_pk PRIMARY KEY  (id)
);
```

Please notice a few things:

NOT NULL -> This is a property telling us that this column can't be empty (must be defined)

IDENTITY (1, 1) -> is also a property of the column telling us that this value shall be generated automatically, starting from 1 and increasing by 1 for each new record

CONSTRAINT city_pk PRIMARY KEY (id) -> This is not a column, but the rule, telling us that column id shall contain only UNIQUE values. So only 1 city can have id =5

-- Table: country

```
CREATE TABLE country (

    id int  NOT NULL IDENTITY(1, 1),

    country_name char(128)  NOT NULL,

    country_name_eng char(128)  NOT NULL,

    country_code char(8)  NOT NULL,

    CONSTRAINT country_ak_1 UNIQUE (country_name),

    CONSTRAINT country_ak_2 UNIQUE (country_name_eng),

    CONSTRAINT country_ak_3 UNIQUE (country_code),

    CONSTRAINT country_pk PRIMARY KEY (id)
);
```

Here we have 1 new CONSTRAINT, and that is the UNIQUE constraining. This one tells us that this value must be UNIQUE within this table. E.g., CONSTRAINT country_ak_1 UNIQUE (country_name) defines that we can't store 2 countries with the same name.

The last part of the script is the definition of foreign keys. We have only 1 such key, and it relates to the city and country table (city.county_id = country.id).

-- foreign keys

-- Reference: city_country (table: city)

```
ALTER TABLE city ADD CONSTRAINT city_country

    FOREIGN KEY (country_id)
```

REFERENCES country (id);

CHAPTER SIX

WHAT ARE SQL SERVER DATA TYPES?

Before we get into the info types utilized in SQL server, I feel it's important for everybody to know what a data type is, and why they're needed to be used in computers.

For our example, we'll mention an individual. If you were brooding about the knowledge you'd use to explain an individual, you'll think to gather their name, birthdate, weight, and number of youngsters. For each of those attributes, the info generally falls into several categories.

Names are stored as text, birthdates as calendar dates, and weight as decimal values, and variety of youngsters as integers. Each of those categories of values may be a data type.

How SQL Types Help

Data types define the characteristics of the info, which will be stored during a location like a database column. A knowledge type defines the possible set of values that are accepted. For instance, a kind of INT which stands for integer in SQL server can only accept whole numbers; decimal values aren't allowed.

When age is defined as an integer, the expectation is data are entered as whole numbers.

Also, without stepping into technical details, you'll see storing the age as an integer takes up much less space than the age within the first table. This might not appear to be an enormous consideration with small databases, but when working with data on smartphones or "big data" scenarios, these considerations add up.

Once the system understands the info type, it can then sort the info in an order that creates sense also as perform calculations.

Reasons to use SQL Server Data Types

Here are some reasons why data types are important:

- Data is stored during a consistent and known format.
- Knowing the info type allows you to understand which calculations and formulations you'll use on the column.
- Data types affect storage. Some values take up more room when stored in one data type versus another. Take our age tables above, for instance.
- Data types affect performance. The less time the database has got to infer values or convert them, the higher. "Is December 32, 2015, a date?"

Commonly used SQL Server Data Types

In SQL, you define what quite data to store within columns. Some example includes text or numeric data.

This is the column's data type, and during all |one amongst |one in every of"> one among its most vital properties because it alone determines whether a worth is valid for storage in a column.

There are over thirty different data types. You'll choose between when defining columns; some have specific uses, like storing images.

The seven data types you'll most often encounter in your everyday use of SQL. These are:

- INT
- VARCHAR
- NVARCHAR
- DATETIME
- DECIMAL
- FLOAT
- BIT

INT – Integer Data Type

The integer data type stores whole numbers. Examples include -23, 0, 5, and 10045. Whole numbers don't include decimal places. Since the SQL server uses a variety of computer words to represent an integer, there are maximum and minimum values that it can represent. An INT data type can store a worth from -2,147,483,648 to 2,147,483,647.

Practical uses of the INT data type include using it to count values, store a person's age, or use it as an ID key to a table.

But INT wouldn't be so good to stay track of a terabyte disk drive address space, because the INT data type only goes to 2 billion and that we would wish to trace into the trillions. For this, you'll use BIGINT.

VARCHAR and NVARCHAR – Text Values

Use VARCHAR and NVARCHAR to store variable-length text values. "VARCHAR" stands for variable-length character.

What makes VARCHAR popular is that values but fifty characters take less space. Space is allocated as required. This differs from the CHAR data type, which always allocates the required length, no matter the length of the particular data stored.

The VARCHAR data type can typically store a maximum of 8,000 characters. Use the NVARCHAR datatype to store Unicode text. Since UNICODE characters occupy twice the space, NVARCHAR columns can store a maximum of 4,000 characters.

The advantage NVARCHAR has over VARCHAR is it can store Unicode characters. This makes it handy to store extended character sets like those used for languages like Kanji.

Databases designed before SQL 2008 typically use VARCHAR; however, more modern databases or those global in nature tend to use NVARCHAR.

DATETIME – Date and Time

Use the DATETIME data type to store the date and time. An example of a DATETIME value is 1968-10-23 1:45:37.123

This is the worth for October 23rd, 1968, at 1:45 AM. Actually, time is more precise than that. The time is basically 45 minutes, 37.123 seconds.

In many cases, you only got to store the date. In these cases, the time component is zeroed out. Thus, November 5th, 1972 is 1972-11-05 00:00:00.000

A DATETIME can store dates from January 1, 1753, through New Year's Eve, 9999. This makes the DATETIME good for recording dates in today's world, but not such a lot in William Shakespeare's.

As you get more conversant in the varied SQL built-in functions, you'll be ready to manipulate the info. To offer you a glimpse, we'll use the YEAR function to count employees hired annually. When given a DATETIME value, the YEAR function returns the year.

DECIMAL and FLOAT – Decimal Points

Use both DECIMAL and FLOAT datatypes to figure with decimal values like 10.3.

I lumped DECIMAL and FLOAT into an equivalent category since they both can handle values with decimal points; however, they both do so differently:

If you would like precise values, like when working with financial or data, then use DECIMAL. The rationale is that the DECIMAL datatype allows you to define the number of decimal points to take care of.

DECIMAL

DECIMAL data types are defined by precision and scale. The precision determines the number of total digits to store; whereas, scale determines the number of digits to the proper of the percentage point.

A DECIMAL data type is specified as DECIMAL (precision, scale).

A DECIMAL data type is often no quite 38 digits. The precision and scale must adhere to the subsequent relation 0

CHAPTER SEVEN

LEARN INPUT DATA INTO A DATABASE

Data is inserted into a table using the INSERT INTO command. This command allows the choice to include a single line in the existing base or several lines at once.

Inserting one line at a time

To insert data into a database, there are two main syntaxes:

Insert a row indicating the information for each existing column (in order)

Insert a row by specifying the columns you wish to complete. It is possible to insert a line filling only part of the columns

Insert row specifying all columns

The syntax for filling a line with this method is as follows:

INSERT INTO VALUES table ('value 1', 'value 2', ...)

This syntax has the following advantages and disadvantages:

Obligation to fill in all the data, while respecting the order of the columns

There is no column name, so typos are limited. In addition, columns can be renamed without having to change the query

The order of the columns must remain identical otherwise certain values take the risk of being completed in the wrong column

Insert a row by specifying only the desired columns

This second solution is very similar, except that you must indicate the name of the columns before "VALUES." The syntax is as follows:

INSERT INTO table (column_name_1, column_name_2, ...

 VALUES ('value 1', 'value 2', ...)

Note: it is possible not to fill in all the columns. In addition, the order of the columns is not important.

Inserting multiple lines at once

It is possible to add several rows to a table with a single query. To do this, use the following syntax: INSERT INTO client (first name, last name, city, age)

 VALUES

 ('Rébecca', 'Armand', 'Saint-Didier-des-Bois', 24),

 ('Aimée', 'Hebert', 'Marigny-le-Châtel', 36),

 ('Marielle', 'Ribeiro', 'Maillères', 27),

 ('Hilaire', 'Savary', 'Conie-Molitard', 58);

Please note: when the field to be filled is of VARCHAR or TEXT type, the text must be indicated in single quotes. On the other hand, when the column is a numeric such as INT or BIGINT, there is no need to use a quotation mark; you just have to indicate the number.

Insert data

This chapter is devoted to inserting data into a table. Nothing too complicated, but it is obviously crucial. Indeed, what would a database be without data?

We will see, among others:

- how to insert a row in a table;
- how to insert several rows in a table;
- how to execute SQL queries written in a file (insert queries or others);
- how to insert in a table line defined in a file of a particular format.

And to finish, we will populate our Animal table with around sixty little critters on which

we can test all kinds of requests in the rest of this tutorial. evil:

INSERT syntax

Two possibilities are available to us when we want to insert a row in a table: either give a value for each column of the row or give the values only of certain columns, in which case it is, of course, necessary to specify which columns it's about.

Insert without specifying columns

I remind for the distracted that our Animal table is composed of six columns: id, species, sex, date of birth, name, and comments.

Here is the syntax to use to insert a line in Animal, without entering the columns for which we give a value (implicitly, MySQL considers that we give a value for each column of the table).

INSERT INTO Animal

VALUES (1, 'chien', 'M', '2010-04-05 13:43:00', 'Rox', 'Mordille beaucoup');

Second example: this time, we do not know the sex, and we have no comments to make on the beast.

INSERT INTO Animal

VALUES (2, 'chat', NULL, '2010-03-24 02:23:00', 'Roucky', NULL);

Third and last example: we give the NULL value of id, which in principle is impossible since id is defined as NOT NULL and as the primary key. However, the auto-incrementation makes that MySQL will calculate on its own as a big one, which id should be given to the line (here: 3).

INSERT INTO Animal

VALUES (NULL, 'chat', 'F', '2010-09-13 15:02:00', 'Schtroumpfette', NULL);

You now have three animals in your table:

Id	Species	Sex	Date of Birth	Last name	Comments
1	Dog	M	2010-04-05 13:43:00	Rox	Nibbles a lot
2	Cat	NULL	2010-03-24 02:23:00	Roucky	NULL
3	Cat	F	2010-09-13 15:02:00	Smurfette	NULL

To verify, you can use the following query:

SELECT * FROM Animal;

Two important things to remember here:

an id is a number, so we don't put quotes around it. However, the species, name, date of birth, and sex are given in the form of character strings. Quotation marks are, therefore, essential. As for NULL, it is an SQL marker which, I remind you, means "no value." No quotes, therefore.

The values of the columns are given in the correct order (therefore, in the order given when the table was created). This is essential, of course. If you exchange the name and the species, for example, how could MySQL know?

Insertion by specifying the columns

In the query, we will, therefore, explicitly write to which column (s) we give value. This will do two things:

The values should no longer be given in the order in which the columns were created, but in the order specified by the query.

We no longer have to give a value to each column; no more need NULL when you have no value to put.

Some examples:

INSERT INTO Animal (espece, sexe, date_naissance)

   VALUES ('tortue', 'F', '2009-08-03 05:12:00');

INSERT INTO Animal (nom, commentaires, date_naissance, espece)

   VALUES ('Choupi', 'Né sans oreille gauche', '2010-10-03 16:44:00', 'chat');

INSERT INTO Animal (espece, date_naissance, commentaires, nom, sexe)

   VALUES ('tortue', '2009-06-13 08:17:00', 'Carapace bizarre', 'Bobosse', 'F');

Which gives you three additional animals (so six in all, you have to follow!)

Multiple insertion

If you have several lines to enter, you can do it in a single request as follows:

INSERT INTO Animal (espece, sexe, date_naissance, nom)

VALUES ('chien', 'F', '2008-12-06 05:18:00', 'Caroline'),

      ('chat', 'M', '2008-09-11 15:38:00', 'Bagherra'),

      ('tortue', NULL, '2010-08-23 05:18:00', NULL);

Of course, you are then obliged to specify the same columns for each entry, even if it means putting NULL some. But admit that it still does less to write!

Alternative MySQL Syntax

MySQL offers an alternative syntax INSERT INTO ... VALUES ... to insert data into a table.

INSERT INTO Animal

SET nom='Bobo', espece='chien', sexe='M', date_naissance='2010-07-21 15:41:00';

This syntax has two advantages.

Having the column and the value assigned to it (nom = 'Bobo') next to each other makes the syntax more readable and easier to handle. Indeed, here, there are only six columns, but imagine a table with 20, even 100 columns. Difficult to be sure that the order in which we declared the columns is the same as the order of the values we give them…

It is very similar to the syntax of UPDATE, which we will see later and which allows modifying existing data. It is, therefore, fewer things to remember (but hey, one request more or less, it is not huge either …).

However, this alternative syntax also has flaws, which for me, are more important than the advantages. That is why I do not recommend using it. I show it to you, especially so that you won't be surprised if you meet it somewhere.

This syntax has two major flaws.

It is specific to MySQL. It is not pure SQL. Therefore, if you ever decide to migrate your database to another RDBMS, you will have to rewrite all the requests INSERT using this syntax.

It does not allow multiple insertions.

Use of external files

Now that you know how to insert data, I suggest you fill this table a bit so that we can have fun later.
Rest assured, I am not going to ask you to invent fifty critters and write one by one the queries to insert them. I pre-chewed the job for you. In addition, it will allow us to have the same thing for you and me in our database. This will make it easier to verify that your requests are doing the right thing.
And to avoid writing all the insertion requests yourself, let's see how we can use a text file to interact with our database.

Execute SQL commands from a file

Writing all the commands by hand into the console can quickly become tedious when it's a small request, no problem. But when you have a long request or a lot of requests, it can be quite long.

A nice solution is to write the queries in a text file, then tell MySQL to execute the queries contained in this file. And to tell him that it's easy:

SOURCE monFichier.sql;

Or

\. monFichier.sql;

These two commands are equivalent and will execute the file monFichier.sql. It is not essential to give it the extension .sql, but I prefer to do it to locate my SQL files directly. In addition, if you use a slightly more advanced text editor than notepad (or

TextEdit on Mac), this will color your SQL code, which will also make things easier for you.

Warning: if you do not give it the path, MySQL will search for your file in the folder where you were when you connected.

Example: we give the full path to the file.

SOURCE Users\taguan\dossierX\monFichier.sql;

If you are using Windows, use "/" instead of "\."

SOURCE C: / "Document and Settings" /dossierX/monFichier.sql;

Insert data from a formatted file

By formatted file, I mean a file that follows certain format rules. A typical example would be .csv files. These files contain a certain amount of data and are organized in tables. Each row corresponds to entry, and the columns of the table are separated by a defined character (often a comma or a semicolon). This, for example, is a CSV format:

nom;prenom;date_naissance

Charles; Myeur;1994-12-30

Bruno;Debor;1978-05-12

Mireille; Franelli;1990-08-23

This type of file is easy to produce (and read) with spreadsheet software (Microsoft Excel, ExcelViewer, Numbers, etc.). The good news is that it is also possible to read this type of file with MySQL, in order to fill a table with the data contained in the file. The SQL command for doing this is LOAD DATA INFILE, here is the syntax:

LOAD DATA [LOCAL] INFILE 'nom_fichier'

INTO TABLE nom_table

[FIELDS

   [TERMINATED BY '\t']

   [ENCLOSED BY ''']

   [ESCAPED BY '\\']

]

[LINES

   [STARTING BY '']

   [TERMINATED BY '\n']

]

[IGNORE nombre LINES]

[(nom_colonne,...)];

The keyword is LOCAL used to specify whether the file is on the client-side (in this case, we use LOCAL) or on the server-side (in which case, we do not put LOCAL in the command). If the file is on the server-side, it is mandatory, for security reasons, that it is in the database directory, that is to say in the directory created by MySQL when creating the database, which contains the files in which the database data are stored. For my part, I will always use LOCAL, in order to be able to simply put my files in my working folder.

The clauses FIELDS and LINES allow us to define the file format used. FIELDS refers to columns, and LINES to the lines (if yes). These two clauses are optional. The values that I put above are the default values.

If you specify a clause FIELDS, you must give it at least one of the three "sub-clauses."

TERMINATED BY, which defines the character separating the columns, between quotes, of course. '\t' corresponds to a tabulation. It is the default character.

ENCLOSED BY, which defines the character surrounding the values in each column (empty by default).

ESCAPED BY, which defines the escape character for special characters. If, for example, you define your values as surrounded by apostrophes, but that certain values contain apostrophes, it is necessary to escape these "internal" apostrophes so that they are not considered as a beginning or an end of the value. By default, this is the \usual. Note that it must itself be dropped in the clause.

Likewise, for LINES, if you use it, you must give it one or two sub-clauses.

STARTING BY, which defines the line start character (empty by default).

TERMINATED BY, which defines the end of line character ('\n' by default, but beware, files generated under Windows often have the '\r\n' end of line character).

The clause IGNORE Nombre LINES allows… to ignore a certain number of lines. For example, if the files first line contains the names of the columns, you do not want to insert it in your table. Then just use IGNORE 1 LINES.

Finally, you can specify the name of the columns present in your file. Be careful, of course, that the missing columns accept NULL or are auto-incremented.

I take my example again, imagining that we have a Person table containing the columns id (auto-incremented primary key), name, first name, date_birth, and address (which can be NULL).

nom;prenom;date_naissance

Charles; Myeur;1994-12-30

Bruno;Debor;1978-05-12

Mireille; Franelli;1990-08-23

If this file is saved under the name personne.csv, you just need to execute the following command to save these three lines in the Person table, specifying if necessary the full path to personne.csv:

LOAD DATA LOCAL INFILE 'personne.csv.'

INTO TABLE Personne

FIELDS TERMINATED BY ';'

LINES TERMINATED BY '\n' -- ou '\r\n' Selon l'ordinateur et le program utilisés pour créer le Fichier

IGNORE 1 line

(nom,prenom,date_naissance);

Filling the base

We are going to use the two techniques I have just shown to fill our database a bit. Don't forget to modify the commands given to add the path to your files.

Execution of SQL commands

Here is the code that I ask you to copy and paste into your favorite text editor, then save under the name fillingAnimal.sql (or another name of your choice).

INSERT INTO Animal (sex, date_naissance, nom, comment) VALUES

1) ('chien', 'F', '2008-02-20 15:45:00' , 'Canaille', NULL),
2) ('chien', 'F','2009-05-26 08:54:00' , 'Cali', NULL),
3) ('chien', 'F','2007-04-24 12:54:00' , 'Rouquine', NULL),
4) ('chien', 'F','2009-05-26 08:56:00' , 'Fila', NULL),
5) ('chien', 'F','2008-02-20 15:47:00' , 'Anya', NULL),
6) ('chien', 'F','2009-05-26 08:50:00' ,'Louya' , NULL),
7) ('chien', 'F', '2008-03-10 13:45:00','Welva' , NULL),
8) ('chien', 'F','2007-04-24 12:59:00' ,'Zira' , NULL),
9) ('chien', 'F', '2009-05-26 09:02:00','Java' , NULL),
10) ('chien', 'M','2007-04-24 12:45:00' ,'Balou' , NULL),
11) ('chien', 'M','2008-03-10 13:43:00' ,'Pataud' , NULL),
12) ('chien', 'M','2007-04-24 12:42:00' , 'Bouli', NULL),
13) ('chien', 'M', '2009-03-05 13:54:00','Zoulou' , NULL),
14) ('chien', 'M','2007-04-12 05:23:00' ,'Cartouche' , NULL),
15) ('chien', 'M', '2006-05-14 15:50:00', 'Zambo', NULL),
16) ('chien', 'M','2006-05-14 15:48:00' ,'Samba' , NULL),
17) ('chien', 'M', '2008-03-10 13:40:00','Moka' , NULL),
18) ('chien', 'M', '2006-05-14 15:40:00','Pilou' , NULL),
19) ('chat', 'M','2009-05-14 06:30:00' , 'Fiero', NULL),
20) ('chat', 'M','2007-03-12 12:05:00' ,'Zonko', NULL),
21) ('chat', 'M','2008-02-20 15:45:00' , 'Filou', NULL),
22) ('chat', 'M','2007-03-12 12:07:00' , 'Farceur', NULL),
23) ('chat', 'M','2006-05-19 16:17:00' ,'Caribou' , NULL),

24) ('chat', 'M','2008-04-20 03:22:00' , 'Capou', NULL),
25) ('chat', 'M','2006-05-19 16:56:00' , 'Raccou', 'Pas de queue depuis la naissance');

You just have to type:

SOURCE remplissageAnimal.sql;

LOAD DATA INFILE

Again, copy and paste the text below into your text editor and save the file. This time under the name animal.csv.

1) "chat";"M";"2009-05-14 06:42:00";"Boucan";NULL
2) "chat";"F";"2006-05-19 16:06:00";"Callune";NULL
3) "chat";"F";"2009-05-14 06:45:00";"Boule";NULL
4) "chat";"F";"2008-04-20 03:26:00";"Zara";NULL
5) "chat";"F";"2007-03-12 12:00:00";"Milla";NULL
6) "chat";"F";"2006-05-19 15:59:00";"Feta";NULL
7) "chat";"F";"2008-04-20 03:20:00";"Bilba";"Sourde de l'oreille droite à 80%"
8) "chat";"F";"2007-03-12 11:54:00";"Cracotte";NULL
9) "chat";"F";"2006-05-19 16:16:00";"Cawette";NULL
10) "tortue";"F";"2007-04-01 18:17:00";"Nikki";NULL
11) "tortue";"F";"2009-03-24 08:23:00";"Tortilla";NULL
12) "tortue";"F";"2009-03-26 01:24:00";"Scroupy";NULL
13) "tortue";"F";"2006-03-15 14:56:00";"Lulla";NULL
14) "tortue";"F";"2008-03-15 12:02:00";"Dana";NULL
15) "tortue";"F";"2009-05-25 19:57:00";"Cheli";NULL
16) "tortue";"F";"2007-04-01 03:54:00";"Chicaca";NULL
17) "tortue";"F";"2006-03-15 14:26:00";"Redbul";"Insomniaque"
18) "tortue";"M";"2007-04-02 01:45:00";"Spoutnik";NULL
19) "tortue";"M";"2008-03-16 08:20:00";"Bubulle";NULL
20) "tortue";"M";"2008-03-15 18:45:00";"Relou";"Surpoids"
21) "tortue";"M";"2009-05-25 18:54:00";"Bulbizard";NULL
22) "perroquet";"M";"2007-03-04 19:36:00";"Safran";NULL
23) "perroquet";"M";"2008-02-20 02:50:00";"Gingko";NULL
24) "perroquet";"M";"2009-03-26 08:28:00";"Bavard";NULL
25) "perroquet";"F";"2009-03-26 07:55:00";"Parlotte";NULL

Attention, the file must end with a line break!

CHAPTER EIGHT

HOW TO SELECT DATA FROM SQL TABLES

SELECT

A simple SELECT statement is the most basic way to query multiple tables. You can call more than one table in the FROM clause to combine results from multiple tables. Here's an example of how this works:

SELECT table1.column1, table2.column2 FROM table1, table2 WHERE table1.column1 = table2.column1;

In this example, I used dot notation (table1.column1) to specify which table the column came from. If the column in question only appears in one of the referenced tables, you don't need to include the fully qualified name, but it may be useful to do so for readability.

Tables are separated in the FROM clause by commas. You can include as many tables as needed, although some databases have a limit to what they can efficiently handle before introducing a formal JOIN statement, which is described below.

This syntax is, in effect, a simple INNER JOIN. Some databases treat it exactly the same as an explicit JOIN. The WHERE clause tells the database which fields to correlate, and it returns results as if the tables listed were combined into a single table based on the provided conditions. It's worth noting that your conditions for comparison don't have to be the same columns you return as your result set. In the example above, table1.column1 and table2.column1 are used to combine the tables, but table2.column2 is returned.

You can extend this functionality to more than two tables using AND keywords in the WHERE clause. You can also use such a combination of tables to restrict your results without actually returning columns from every table. In the example below, table3 is matched up with table1, but I haven't returned anything from table3 for display. I've merely checked to make sure the relevant column from table1 exists in table3. Note that table3 needs to be referenced in the FROM clause for this example.
SELECT table1.column1, table2.column2 FROM table1, table2, table3 WHERE table1.column1 = table2.column1 AND table1.column1 = table3.column1;

Be warned, however, that this method of querying multiple tables is effectively an implied JOIN. Your database may handle things differently, depending on the optimization engine it uses. Also, neglecting to define the nature of the correlation with a WHERE clause can give you undesirable results, such as returning the rogue field in a column associated with every possible result from the rest of the query, as in a CROSS JOIN.

If you're comfortable with how your database handles this type of statement, and you're combining two or just a few tables, a simple SELECT statement will meet your needs.

CHAPTER NINE

HOW TO USE AGGREGATE FUNCTIONS

Aggregate functions in SQL

As the Basic SQL Tutorial points out, SQL is superb at aggregating data the way you would possibly during a pivot table in Excel. You'll use aggregate functions all the time, so it is vital to urge comfortable with them. The functions themselves are equivalent ones you'll find in Excel or the other analytics program. We'll cover them individually within the next few lessons. Here's a fast preview:

COUNT counts what number rows are during a particular column.

SUM adds together all the values during a particular column.

MIN and MAX return rock bottom and highest values during a particular column, respectively.

AVG calculates the typical of a gaggle of selected values.

The Basic SQL Tutorial also acknowledged that arithmetic operators only perform operations across rows. Aggregate functions are wont to perform operations across entire columns (which could include many rows of knowledge or more).

Like most other relational database products, PostgreSQL ™ supports aggregate functions. An aggregate function calculates a single result from multiple input lines. For example, there are aggregates to calculate the number (count), sum (sum), mean (avg), maximum (max), and minimum (min) of a set of lines.

As an example, we can find the highest temperature among the low temperatures with:

SELECT max (t_bass) FROM time;

 max

 46

(1 row)

If we want to know in which city (or cities) these readings occurred, we can try

SELECT city FROM time WHERE t_basse = max (t_basse);

FALSE

but it will not work since the max aggregate cannot be used in a WHERE clause (this restriction exists because the WHERE clause determines which rows will be processed by the aggregate; therefore, the rows must be evaluated before the functions d 'aggregate calculate). However, as is often the case, the query can be repeated to achieve the expected result, here using a subquery :

SELECT city FROM time

    WHERE t_basse = (SELECT max (t_basse) FROM time);

    city

 San Francisco

(1 row)

This is correct because the subquery is an independent calculation that treats its own aggregate separately from what happens in the external query.

Aggregates are also very useful if they are combined with GROUP BY clauses. For example, we can obtain the highest temperature among the low temperatures observed in each city with

SELECT city, max (t_basse)

   FROM time

   GROUP BY city;

   city | max

---------------- + -----

Hayward | 37

San Francisco | 46

(2 rows)

which gives us one line per city in the result. Each aggregate result is calculated with the rows of the table corresponding to the city. We can filter these grouped lines using HAVING:

SELECT city, max (t_basse)

   FROM time

   GROUP BY city

   HAVING max (t_bass) <40;

  city | max

--------- + -----

Hayward | 37

(1 row)

which gives us the same result only for cities that have all their t_bass values below 40. Finally, if we only care about cities whose names start with " S, "we can do

SELECT city, max (t_basse)

   FROM time

   WHERE city LIKE 'S%'

   GROUP BY city

   HAVING max (t_bass) <40;

It is important to understand the interaction between aggregates and the SQL WHERE and HAVING clauses. The fundamental difference between WHERE and HAVING is that WHERE selects the input lines before the groups and aggregates are processed (therefore, this clause controls the lines that are found in the calculation of the aggregate) while HAVING selected the lines grouped after groups and aggregates have been processed. So the WHERE clause must not contain aggregate functions; it makes no sense to try to use an aggregate to determine which rows will be input to the aggregates. On the other hand, the HAVING clause always contains aggregate functions (to be precise, you are allowed to write a HAVING clause that does not use aggregates, but it is rarely used. The same condition can be used more effectively by a WHERE).

In the previous example, we can apply the restriction on the name of the city in WHERE since this does not require any aggregate. This is more efficient than adding the restriction in HAVING because we avoid grouping and aggregate calculations for all the rows which failed during the check made by WHERE.

CHAPTER TEN

HOW TO WRITE JOIN AND UNION STATEMENTS

SQL JOIN

A JOIN clause is used to combine rows from two or more tables, based on a related column between them.

Let's look at a selection from the "Orders" table:

OrderID	CustomerID	OrderDate
10308	2	1996-09-18
10309	37	1996-09-19
10310	77	1996-09-20

Then, look at a selection from the "Customers" table:

CustomerID	CustomerName	ContactName
1	Alfreds Futterkiste	Maria Anders
2	Ana Trujillo Emparedados y helados	Ana Trujillo
3	Antonio Moreno Taquería	Antonio Moreno

Notice that the "CustomerID" column in the "Orders" table refers to the "CustomerID" in the "Customers" table. The relationship between the two tables above is the "CustomerID" column.

Then, we can create the following SQL statement (that contains an INNER JOIN), that selects records that have matching values in both tables:

Example

```
SELECT Orders.OrderID, Customers.CustomerName, Orders.OrderDate
FROM Orders
INNER JOIN Customers ON Orders.CustomerID=Customers.CustomerID;
```

SQL INNER JOIN Keyword

The INNER JOIN keyword selects records that have matching values in both tables.

INNER JOIN Syntax

```
SELECT column_name(s)
FROM table1
INNER JOIN table2
ON table1.column_name = table2.column_name;
```

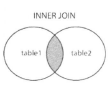

INNER JOIN

table1   table2

Below is a selection from the "Orders" table:

And a selection from the "Customers" table:

CustomerID	CustomerName	ContactName	Address
1	Alfreds Futterkiste	Maria Anders	Obere Str. 57
2	Ana Trujillo Emparedados y helados	Ana Trujillo	Avda. de la Constituc:
3	Antonio Moreno Taquería	Antonio Moreno	Mataderos 2312

SQL INNER JOIN

Example

The following SQL statement selects all orders with customer information:

Example

```
SELECT Orders.OrderID, Customers.CustomerName
FROM Orders
INNER JOIN Customers ON Orders.CustomerID = Customers.CustomerID;
```

The INNER JOIN keyword selects all rows from both tables as long as there is a match between the columns. If there are records in the "Orders" table that do not have matches in "Customers," these orders will not be shown!

SQL LEFT JOIN Keyword

The LEFT JOIN keyword returns all records from the left table (table1), and the matched records from the right table (table2). The result is NULL from the right side if there is no match.

LEFT JOIN Syntax

```
SELECT column_name(s)
FROM table1
LEFT JOIN table2
ON table1.column_name = table2.column_name;
```

Note: In some databases, LEFT JOIN is called LEFT OUTER JOIN.

LEFT JOIN

Demo Database

In this tutorial, we will use the well-known Northwind sample database.

Below is a selection from the "Customers" table:

CustomerID	CustomerName	ContactName	Address
1	Alfreds Futterkiste	Maria Anders	Obere Str. 57
2	Ana Trujillo Emparedados y helados	Ana Trujillo	Avda. de la Constitución
3	Antonio Moreno Taquería	Antonio Moreno	Mataderos 2312

And a selection from the "Orders" table:

OrderID	CustomerID	EmployeeID	OrderDate
10308	2	7	1996-09-18
10309	37	3	1996-09-19
10310	77	8	1996-09-20

SQL LEFT JOIN

Example

The following SQL statement will select all customers, and any orders they might have:

Example

```
SELECT Customers.CustomerName, Orders.OrderID
FROM Customers
LEFT JOIN Orders ON Customers.CustomerID = Orders.CustomerID
ORDER BY Customers.CustomerName;
```

SQL RIGHT JOIN Keyword

The RIGHT JOIN keyword returns all records from the right table (table2), and the matched records from the left table (table1). The result is NULL from the left side when there is no match.

RIGHT JOIN Syntax

```
SELECT column_name(s)
FROM table1
RIGHT JOIN table2
ON table1.column_name = table2.column_name;
```

Note: In some databases, RIGHT JOIN is called RIGHT OUTER JOIN.

RIGHT JOIN

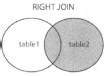

Below is a selection from the "Orders" table:

OrderID	CustomerID	EmployeeID	OrderDate
10308	2	7	1996-09-1:
10309	37	3	1996-09-1'
10310	77	8	1996-09-2(

And a selection from the "Employees" table:

EmployeeID	LastName	FirstName	BirthDat(
1	Davolio	Nancy	12/8/196:

| 2 | Fuller | Andrew | 2/19/1952 |
| 3 | Leverling | Janet | 8/30/1963 |

SQL RIGHT JOIN

Example

The following SQL statement will return all employees, and any orders they might have placed:

Example

```
SELECT Orders.OrderID, Employees.LastName, Employees.FirstName
FROM Orders
RIGHT JOIN Employees ON Orders.EmployeeID = Employees.EmployeeID
ORDER BY Orders.OrderID;
```

SQL FULL OUTER JOIN Keyword

The FULL OUTER JOIN keyword returns all records when there are a match in left (table1) or right (table2) table records.

Note: FULL OUTER JOIN can potentially return very large result-sets!

Tip: FULL OUTER JOIN and FULL JOIN are the same.

FULL OUTER JOIN Syntax

```
SELECT column_name(s)
FROM table1
FULL OUTER JOIN table2
ON table1.column_name = table2.column_name
WHERE condition;
```

FULL OUTER JOIN

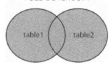

Demo Database

In this tutorial, we will use the well-known Northwind sample database.

Below is a selection from the "Customers" table:

CustomerID	CustomerName	ContactName	Address
1	Alfreds Futterkiste	Maria Anders	Obere Str. 57
2	Ana Trujillo Emparedados y helados	Ana Trujillo	Avda. de la Constituci
3	Antonio Moreno Taquería	Antonio Moreno	Mataderos 2312

And a selection from the "Orders" table:

OrderID	CustomerID	EmployeeID	OrderDate
10308	2	7	1996-09-1:
10309	37	3	1996-09-1!
10310	77	8	1996-09-2(

SQL FULL OUTER JOIN

Example

The following SQL statement selects all customers and all orders:

SELECT Customers.CustomerName, Orders.OrderID
FROM Customers
FULL OUTER JOIN Orders ON Customers.CustomerID=Orders.CustomerID
ORDER BY Customers.CustomerName;

A selection from the result set may look like this:

CustomerName
Alfreds Futterkiste
Ana Trujillo Emparedados y helados
Antonio Moreno Taquería

Note: The FULL OUTER JOIN keyword returns all matching records from both tables, whether the other table matches or not. So, if there are rows in "Customers" that do not have matches in "Orders," or if there are rows in "Orders" that do not have matches in "Customers," those rows will be listed as well.

SQL Self JOIN

A self-JOIN is a regular join, but the table is joined with itself.

Self-JOIN Syntax

```
SELECT column_name(s)
FROM table1 T1, table1 T2
WHERE condition;
```

T1 and T2 are different table aliases for the same table.

Demo Database

In this tutorial, we will use the well-known Northwind sample database.

Below is a selection from the "Customers" table:

CustomerID	CustomerName	ContactName	Address
1	Alfreds Futterkiste	Maria Anders	Obere Str. 57
2	Ana Trujillo Emparedados y helados	Ana Trujillo	Avda. de la Constitución
3	Antonio Moreno Taquería	Antonio Moreno	Mataderos 2312

SQL Self JOIN Example

The following SQL statement matches customers that are from the same city:

Example

```
SELECT A.CustomerName AS CustomerName1,
B.CustomerName AS CustomerName2, A.City
FROM Customers A, Customers B
WHERE A.CustomerID <> B.CustomerID
AND A. City = B.City
ORDER BY A.City;
```

JOIN works in the same way as the SELECT statement above—it returns a result set with columns from different tables. The advantage of using an explicit JOIN over an implied one is greater control over your result set and possibly improved performance when many tables are involved.

There are several types of JOIN—LEFT, RIGHT, and FULL OUTER; INNER; and CROSS. The type you use is determined by the results you want to see. For example, using a LEFT OUTER JOIN will return all relevant rows from the first table listed, while potentially dropping rows from the second table listed if they don't have information that correlates in the first table.

This differs from an INNER JOIN or an implied JOIN. An INNER JOIN will only return rows for which there is data in both tables.

Use the following JOIN statement for the first SELECT query above:
SELECT table1.column1, table2.column2 FROM table1 INNER JOIN table2
ON table1.column1 = table2.column1;

Subqueries

Subqueries, or subselect statements, is a way to use a result set as a resource in a query. These are often used to limit or refine results rather than run multiple queries or manipulate the data in your application. With a subquery, you can reference tables to determine the inclusion of data or, in some cases, return a column that is the result of a subselect.

The following example uses two tables. One table actually contains the data I'm interested in returning, while the other gives a comparison point to determine what data is actually interesting.
SELECT column1 FROM table1 WHERE EXISTS (SELECT column1 FROM table2
WHERE table1.column1 = table2.column1);

One important factor in subqueries is performance. Convenience comes at a price and, depending on the size, number, and complexity of tables and the statements you use, you may want to allow your application to handle the processing. Each query is processed separately in full before being used as a resource for your primary query. If possible, the creative use of JOIN statements may provide the same information with less lag time.

JOIN statements and subqueries

SQL Subquery

In SQL language, a subquery (also called "nested query" or "cascading query") consists of executing a query inside another query. A nested query is often used within a WHERE or HAVING clause to replace one or more constants.

Syntax

There are several ways to use subqueries. This way, there are several possible syntaxes for using queries in queries.

Nested query that returns a single result

The example below is a typical example of a subquery that returns a single result to the main query.

```
SELECT *
FROM `table`
WHERE `column_name` = (
    SELECT `value`
    FROM `table2`
    LIMIT 1
)
```

This example shows an internal query (the one on "table2"), which returns a single value. As for the external query, it will search for the results from "table" and filter the results from the value returned by the internal query.

Note: it is possible to use any equality operator such as =,>, <,> =, <= or <>.

Nested query that returns a column

A nested query can also return an entire column. Therefore, the external query can use the IN command to filter the rows that have one of the values returned by the internal query. The example below highlights such a scenario:

```
SELECT *
FROM `table.`
WHERE `column_name` IN (
    SELECT `column.`
    FROM `table2.`
    WHERE `cle_etrangere` = 36
)
```

Example

The rest of this article presents concrete examples using subqueries.

Imagine a website that allows you to ask and answer questions. One such site has a database with a table for questions and another for answers.

"Question" table:

q_id	q_date_ajout	q_title	q_content
1	2013-03-24 12:54:32	How to fix a computer?	Hello, my computer is broken, how can I fix it?

q_id	q_date_ajout	q_title	q_content
2	2013-03-26 19:27:41	How to change a tire?	What is the best method to change a tire easily?
3	2013-04-18 20:09:56	What to do if a device is broken?	Is it better to repair electrical appliances or buy new ones?
4	2013-04-22 17:14:27	How to clean a computer keyboard?	Hello, under my computer keyboard there is a lot of dust, how should I proceed to clean it? Thank you.

"Response" table:

r_id	r_fk_question_id	r_date_ajout	r_content
1	1	2013-03-27 07:44:32	Hello. Can you explain what is wrong with your computer? Thank you.
2	1	2013-03-28 19:27:11	Good evening, the easiest way is to hire a professional to repair a computer. Regards,
3	2	2013-05-09 22:10:09	Advice is available on the internet on this subject.
4	3	2013-05-24 09:47:12	Hello. It depends on you, your budget, and your preference for ecology. Regards,

Nested query that returns a single result

With such an application, it may be useful to know the question related to the last answer added to the application. This can be done via the following SQL query:

SELECT *

FROM `question.`

WHERE q_id = (

   SELECT r_fk_question_id

   FROM `answer.`

   ORDER BY r_date_ajout DESC

   LIMIT 1

)

Such a request will return the following line:

q_id	q_date_ajout	q_title	q_content
3	2013-04-18 20:09:56	What to do if a device is broken?	Is it better to repair electrical appliances or buy new ones?

This result shows that the question related to the last answer on the forum is well found from this result.

Nested query that returns a column

Now imagine that we wanted to get the questions related to all the answers between 2 dates. These questions can be retrieved by the following SQL query:

SELECT *

FROM `question.`

WHERE q_id IN (

   SELECT r_fk_question_id

   FROM `answer.`

   WHERE r_date_ajout BETWEEN '2013-01-01' AND '2013-12-31'

)

In our case, this query will return the following results:

q_id	q_date_ajout	q_title	q_content
1	2013-03-24 12:54:32	How to fix a computer?	Hello, my computer is broken, how can I fix it?
2	2013-03-26 19:27:41	How to change a tire?	What is the best method to change a tire easily?
3	2013-04-18 20:09:56	What to do if a device is broken?	Is it better to repair electrical appliances or buy new ones?

Such a request, therefore, makes it possible to retrieve the questions that were answered between 2 dates. This is handy in our case to avoid getting responses that have had no responses at all or no new responses for a long time.

UNION

The UNION statement is another way to return information from multiple tables with a single query. The UNION statement allows you to perform queries against several tables and return the results in a consolidated set, as in the following example.

SELECT column1, column2, column3 FROM table1 UNION SELECT column1, column2, column3 FROM table2;

This will return a result set with three columns containing data from both queries. By default, the UNION statement will omit duplicates between the tables unless the UNION ALL keyword is used. UNION is helpful when the returned columns from the different tables don't have columns or data that can be compared and joined, or when it prevents multiple running queries and appending the results in your application code.

If your column names don't match when you use the UNION statement, use aliases to give your results meaningful headers:
SELECT column1, column2 as Two, column3 as Three FROM table1 UNION SELECT column1, column4 as Two, column5 as Three FROM table2;

As with subqueries, UNION statements can create a heavy load on your database server, but for occasional use, they can save a lot of time.

Multiple options
When it comes to database queries, there are usually many ways to approach the same problem. These are some of the more frequently used methods for consolidating queries on multiple tables into a single statement. While some of these options may affect performance, practice will help you know when it's appropriate to use each type of query.

CHAPTER ELEVEN

WHAT IS A SQL VIEW?

What is a view?

A view is a virtual table, that is to say, the data of which is not stored in a table of the database, and in which it is possible to gather information coming from several tables. We speak of "view" because it is simply a representation of the data for the purpose of visual exploitation. The data present in a view is defined using a SELECT clause.

Creating a view in SQL

The creation of a view is done using the CREATE VIEW clause followed by the name we give to the view, then by the name of the columns whose view we want to enhance (we need as many column redefinitions as there will have output), then finally an AS clause preceding the selection. The syntax of a view, therefore, looks like this:

```
CREATE VIEW View_name
(columns)
AS SELECT ...
```

Here's what it could do:

```
CREATE VIEW View
(columnA, columnB, columnC, columnD)
AS SELECT column1, column2, columnI, columnII
FROM Table_name1 Alias1, Table_nameII AliasII
WHERE Alias1.colonne1 = AliasII.colonneI
AND Alias1.colonne2 = AliasII.columnII
```

The views thus created can be the object of new queries by specifying the name of the view instead of a table name in a SELECT order ...

Interest of views

The view in this way represents a kind of intermediary between the database and the user. This has many consequences:

- a selection of the data to display
- restriction of access to the table for the user, i.e., increased data security
- grouping of information within an entity

A VIEW does not require any storage in a database because it does not exist physically. In a VIEW, we can also control user security for accessing the data from the database tables. We can allow users to get the data from the VIEW, and the user does not require permission for each table or column to fetch data.

Let's explore user-defined VIEW in SQL Server.

Note: I am going to use sample database AdventureWorks for all examples.

Create a SQL VIEW

The syntax to create a VIEW is as follows:

CREATE VIEW Name AS

Select column1, Column2...Column N From tables

Where conditions;

Example 1: SQL VIEW to fetch all records of a table

It is the simplest form of a VIEW. Usually, we do not use a VIEW in SQL Server to fetch all records from a single table.

CREATE VIEW EmployeeRecords

AS

    SELECT *

    FROM [HumanResources].[Employee];

Once a VIEW is created, you can access it like a SQL table.

	BusinessEntityID	NationalIDNumber	LoginID	OrganizationNode	OrganizationLevel	JobTitle	BirthDate	MaritalStatus	Gender
1	1	295847284	adventure-works\ken0	NULL	NULL	search and Development	1969-01-29	S	M
2	2	245797967	adventure-works\terri0	0x58	1	search and Development	1971-08-01	S	F
3	3	509647174	adventure-works\roberto0	0x5AC0	2	search and Development	1974-11-12	M	M
4	4	112457891	adventure-works\rob0	0x5AD6	3	search and Development	1974-12-23	S	M
5	5	695256908	adventure-works\gail0	0x5ADA	3	search and Development	1952-09-27	M	F
6	6	998320692	adventure-works\jossef0	0x5ADE	3	search and Development	1959-03-11	M	M
7	7	134969118	adventure-works\dylan0	0x5AE1	3	search and Development	1987-02-24	M	M
8	8	811994146	adventure-works\diane1	0x5AE158	4	search and Development	1986-06-05	S	F
9	9	658797903	adventure-works\gigi0	0x5AE168	4	search and Development	1979-01-21	M	F
10	10	879342154	adventure-works\michael6	0x5AE178	4	search and Development	1984-11-30	M	M
11	11	974026903	adventure-works\ovidiu0	0x5AE3	3	search and Development	1978-01-17	S	M

Example 2: SQL VIEW to fetch a few columns of a table

We might not be interested in all columns of a table. We can specify required column names in the select statement to fetch those fields only from the table.

CREATE VIEW EmployeeRecords

AS

    SELECT NationalIDNumber,LoginID,JobTitle

    FROM [HumanResources].[Employee];

Example 3: SQL VIEW to fetch a few columns of a table and filter results using WHERE clause

We can filter the results using a Where clause condition in a Select statement. Suppose we want to get EmployeeRecords with Martial status 'M'.

```
CREATE VIEW EmployeeRecords
AS
    SELECT NationalIDNumber,
        LoginID,
        JobTitle,
        MaritalStatus
    FROM [HumanResources].[Employee]
    WHERE MaritalStatus = 'M';
```

Example 4: SQL VIEW to fetch records from multiple tables

We can use a VIEW to have a select statement with Join condition between multiple tables. It is one of the frequent uses of a VIEW in SQL Server.

In the following query, we use INNER JOIN and LEFT OUTER JOIN between multiple tables to fetch a few columns as per our requirement.

```
CREATE VIEW [Sales].[vStoreWithContacts]
AS
    SELECT s.[BusinessEntityID],
        s.[Name],
        ct.[Name] AS [ContactType],
        p.[Title],
        p.[FirstName],
        p.[MiddleName],
        p.[LastName],
        p.[Suffix],
        pp.[PhoneNumber],
        ea.[EmailAddress],
        p.[EmailPromotion]
    FROM [Sales].[Store] s
        INNER JOIN [Person].[BusinessEntityContact] bec ON bec.[BusinessEntityID] = s.[BusinessEntityID]
        INNER JOIN [Person].[ContactType] ct ON ct.[ContactTypeID] = bec.[ContactTypeID]
        INNER JOIN [Person].[Person] p ON p.[BusinessEntityID] = bec.[PersonID]
```

LEFT OUTER JOIN [Person].[EmailAddress] ea ON ea.[BusinessEntityID] = p.[BusinessEntityID]

LEFT OUTER JOIN [Person].[PersonPhone] pp ON pp.[BusinessEntityID] = p.[BusinessEntityID];

GO

Suppose you need to execute this query very frequently. Using a VIEW, we can simply get the data with a single line of code.

select * from [Sales].[vStoreWithContacts]

	BusinessEntityID	Name	ContactType	Title	FirstName	MiddleName	LastName
1	292	Next-Door Bike Store	Owner	Mr.	Gustavo	NULL	Achong
2	294	Professional Sales and Service	Owner	Ms.	Catherine	R.	Abel
3	296	Riders Company	Owner	Ms.	Kim	NULL	Abercrombie
4	298	The Bike Mechanics	Owner	Sr.	Humberto	NULL	Acevedo
5	300	Nationwide Supply	Owner	Sra.	Pilar	NULL	Ackerman
6	302	Area Bike Accessories	Owner	Ms.	Frances	B.	Adams
7	304	Bicycle Accessories and Kits	Owner	Ms.	Margaret	J.	Smith
8	306	Clamps & Brackets Co.	Owner	Ms.	Carla	J.	Adams
9	316	Fun Toys and Bikes	Owner	Mr.	Robert	E.	Ahlering
10	318	Great Bikes	Owner	Mr.	François	NULL	Ferrier
11	320	Metropolitan Sales and Rental	Owner	Ms.	Kim	NULL	Akers

Example 5: SQL VIEW to fetch specific column

In the previous example, we created a VIEW with multiple tables and a few columns from those tables. Once we have a view, it is not required to fetch all columns from the view. We can select few columns as well from a VIEW in SQL Server similar to a relational table.

In the following query, we want to get only two columns name and contract type from the view.

SELECT Name,

ContactType

FROM [Sales].[vStoreWithContacts];

Example 6: Use Sp_helptext to retrieve VIEW definition

We can use sp_helptext system stored procedure to get a VIEW definition. It returns the complete definition of a SQL VIEW.

For example, let's check the view definition for EmployeeRecords VIEW.

```
Text
-----------------------------------------------------------------------------------
CREATE VIEW EmployeeRecords
AS                                    Sp_helptext 'EmployeeRecords'

        SELECT NationalIDNumber,
                LoginID,
                JobTitle,
                MaritalStatus
        FROM [HumanResources].[Employee]
        WHERE MaritalStatus = 'M';
```

We can use SSMS as well to generate the script for a VIEW. Expand database -> Views -> Right click and go to Script view as -> Create To -> New Query Editor Window.

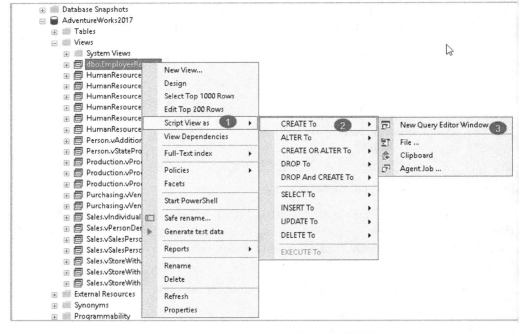

Example 7: sp_refreshview to update the Metadata of a SQL VIEW

Suppose we have a VIEW on a table that specifies select * statement to get all columns of that table.

CREATE VIEW DemoView

AS

    SELECT *

    FROM [AdventureWorks2017].[dbo].[MyTable];

Once we call the VIEW DemoView, it gives the following output.

	TableID	ForeignID	Value	CodeOne	CodeTwo
1	1	1	FooBar	Foo	Bar

Let's add a new column in the table using the Alter table statement.

Alter Table [AdventureWorks2017].[dbo].[MyTable] Add City nvarchar(50)

Rerun the select statement to get records from VIEW. It should display the new column as well in the output. We still get the same output, and it does not contain the newly added column.

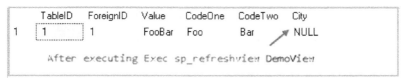

	TableID	ForeignID	Value	CodeOne	CodeTwo
1	1	1	FooBar	Foo	Bar

By default, SQL Server does not modify the schema and metadata for the VIEW. We can use the system stored procedure sp_refreshview to refresh the metadata of any view.

Exec sp_refreshview DemoView

Rerun the select statement to get records from VIEW. We can see the City column in the output.

	TableID	ForeignID	Value	CodeOne	CodeTwo	City
1	1	1	FooBar	Foo	Bar	NULL

After executing Exec sp_refreshview DemoView

Example 8: Schema Binding a SQL VIEW

In the previous example, we modify the SQL table to add a new column. Suppose in the production instance, and you have a view in the application. You are not aware of the changes in the table design for the new column. We do not want any changes to be made in the tables being used in the VIEW. We can use the SCHEMABINDING option to lock all tables used in the VIEW and deny any alter table statement against those tables.

Let's execute the following query with an option SCHEMABINDING.

CREATE VIEW DemoView

WITH SCHEMABINDING

AS

    SELECT *

    FROM [AdventureWorks2017].[dbo].[MyTable];

It gives an error message.

Msg 1054, Level 15, State 6, Procedure DemoView, Line 4 [Batch Start Line 2]
Syntax '*' is not allowed in schema-bound objects.

We cannot call all columns (Select *) in a VIEW with SCHEMABINDING option. Let's specify the columns in the following query and execute it again.

CREATE VIEW DemoView

WITH SCHEMABINDING

AS

    SELECT TableID, ForeignID ,Value, CodeOne

    FROM [AdventureWorks2017].[dbo].[MyTable];

We again get the following error message.

Msg 4512, Level 16, State 3, Procedure DemoView, Line 5 [Batch Start Line 1]
Cannot schema bind VIEW 'DemoView' because of the name
'AdventureWorks2017.dbo.MyTable' is invalid for schema binding.
Names must be in a two-part format, and an object cannot reference itself.

In my query, I used a three-part object name in the format [DBName.Schema.Object]. We cannot use this format with the SCHEMABINDING option in a VIEW. We can use the two-part name as per the following query.

CREATE VIEW DemoView

WITH SCHEMABINDING

AS

    SELECT TableID, ForeignID ,Value, CodeOne

    FROM [dbo].[MyTable];

Once you have created a VIEW with SCHEMABINDING option, try to add a modify a column data type using Alter table command.

ALTER TABLE dbo.MyTable ALTER COLUMN ForeignID
BIGINT;

```
Msg 5074, Level 16, State 1, Line 12
The object 'DemoView' is dependent on column 'ForeignID'.
Msg 4922, Level 16, State 9, Line 12
ALTER TABLE ALTER COLUMN ForeignID failed because one or more objects access this column.
```

We need to drop the VIEW definition itself along with other dependencies on that table before making a change to the existing table schema.

Example 8: SQL VIEW ENCRYPTION

We can encrypt the VIEW using the WITH ENCRYPTION clause. Previously, we checked users can see the view definition using the sp_helptext command. If we do not want users to view the definition, we can encrypt it.

```
CREATE VIEW DemoView

WITH ENCRYPTION

AS

    SELECT TableID, ForeignID ,Value, CodeOne

    FROM [dbo].[MyTable];
```

Now, if you run the sp_helptext command to view the definition, you get the following error message.

Exec sp_helptext DemoView

The text for the object 'DemoView' is encrypted.

Example 9: SQL VIEW for DML (Update, Delete and Insert) queries

We can use SQL VIEW to insert, update, and delete data in a single SQL table. We need to note the following things regarding this.

We can use DML operation on a single table only

VIEW should not contain Group By, Having, Distinct clauses

We cannot use a subquery in a VIEW in SQL Server

We cannot use Set operators in a SQL VIEW

Use the following queries to perform DML operation using VIEW in SQL Server.

Insert DML

        Insert into DemoView values(4,'CC','KK','RR')

Delete DML

        Delete from DemoView where TableID=7

Update DML

        Update DemoView set value='Raj' where TableID=5

Example 10: SQL VIEW and Check Option

We can use the WITH CHECK option to check the conditions in VIEW are inline with the DML statements.

It prevents to insert rows in the table where the condition in the Where clause is not satisfied

If the condition does not satisfy, we get an error message in the insert or update statement

In the following query, we use the CHECK option, and we want only values starting with letter F in the [Codeone] column.

CREATE VIEW DemoView

AS

    SELECT *

    FROM [dbo].[MyTable]

    WHERE [Codeone] LIKE 'F%'

WITH CHECK OPTION;

If we try to insert a value that does not match the condition, we get the following error message.

Insert into DemoView values (5,'CC','Raj','Raj')

```
Msg 550, Level 16, State 1, Line 1
The attempted insert or update failed because the target view either specifies
 WITH CHECK OPTION or spans a view that specifies WITH CHECK OPTION and one or more rows
 resulting from the operation did not qualify under the CHECK OPTION constraint.
The statement has been terminated.
```

Example 11: Drop SQL VIEW

We can drop a VIEW using the DROP VIEW statement. In the following query, we want to drop the VIEW demo view in SQL Server.

DROP VIEW demo
view;

Example 12: Alter a SQL VIEW

We can change the SQL statement in a VIEW using the following alter VIEW command. Suppose we want to change the condition in the where clause of a VIEW. Execute the following query.

Alter VIEW DemoView

AS

    SELECT *

    FROM [dbo].[MyTable]

    WHERE [Codeone] LIKE 'C%'

WITH CHECK OPTION;

Starting from SQL Server 2016 SP1, we can use the CREATE or ALTER statement to create a SQL VIEW or modify it if already exists. Prior to SQL Server 2016 SP1, we cannot use both CREATE or Alter together.

CREATE OR ALTER VIEW
DemoView

AS SELECT *

```
FROM [dbo].[MyTable]
WHERE [Codeone] LIKE 'C%'
WITH CHECK OPTION;
```

CHAPTER TWELVE

HOW TO WRITE SQL TRIGGERS

SQL SERVER CREATE TRIGGER STATEMENT

The CREATE TRIGGER statement allows you to create a new trigger that is fired automatically whenever an event such as INSERT, DELETE, or UPDATE occurs against a table.

Trigger principles

The trigger execution model is based on the event-condition-action (ECA) sequence, which can be described as follows:

a trigger is triggered by an event, specified by the programmer, which is generally an insertion, destruction or modification on a table;

the first action of a trigger is to test a condition: if this condition is not evaluated at TRUE, execution stops;

Finally, the action proper can consist of any set of operations on the database, carried out if necessary, using the procedural language supported by the DBMS.

An important characteristic of this procedure (action) is to be able to simultaneously manipulate the old and new values of the modified data, which makes it possible to make tests on the evolution of the database.

Other important features include the following two. First of all, a trigger can be executed either once for a single SQL order, or for each tuple affected by this order. Then the action taken can occur before the event or after.

The use of triggers makes a database dynamic: an operation on the database can trigger others, which themselves can cause other reflexes to cascade. This mechanism is not without danger because of the risks of an infinite loop.

Take the following example: we want to keep at the table Cinnamate the total number of seats (the sum of the capacity of the rooms). In principle, this is redundancy to avoid in principle, but which can be managed with triggers. We can indeed set up a trigger at the level of Salle, which, for any update, will modify the data at the level Cinema.

Now it's easy to imagine a situation where you end up with cascading triggers. Take the case of a table giving the number of cinema seats in the city. Ville (nom, capacité)

Now suppose that the city manages the time of the first session of a room: we end up with an infinite cycle!

Syntax

The general syntax for creating a trigger is given below.

CREATE [OR REPLACE] TRIGGER <nomTrigger>

 {BEFORE | AFTER}

 {DELETE | INSERT | UPDATE [of column, [, column] ...]}

  [OR {DELETE | INSERT | UPDATE [of column, [, column] ...]}] ...

 ON <nomTable> [FOR EACH ROW]

[WHEN <condition]

   <blocPLSQL>

We can distinguish three parts in this syntactic construction. The event part is specified after BEFORE or AFTER, the condition part after WHEN, and the action part corresponds to the PL / SQL block. Here are some additional explanations of these three parts.

"Event" can be `BEFORE`` or AFTER, followed by DELETE, UPDATEor INSERTseparated by OR.

"Condition" is optional. In its absence, the trigger is triggered once for any request modifying the table, and this without condition. FOR EACH ROW

Otherwise, <condition>is any boolean SQL condition. In addition, you can reference the old and new values of the current tuple with the syntax new.attribut and `` old.attribut`` respectively.

"Action" is a procedure that can be implemented, under Oracle, with the PL / SQL language. It can contain SQL orders but no update of the current table.

The old and new values of the current tuple are referenced by new.attr and: old.attr.

It is possible to modify new and old. For example :new.prix=500;will force the attribute prixto 500 in a BEFORE trigger.

The availability of new and old depends on the context. For example, new is at NULLin, a trigger triggered by DELETE.

Some examples

Here is, first of all, an example of a trigger that maintains the capacity of a cinema with each update on the table Salle.

CREATE TRIGGER CumulCapacite

AFTER UPDATE ON Salle

FOR EACH ROW

WHEN (new.capacite != old.capacite)

BEGIN

  UPDATE Cinema

  SET capacity = capacity - :old.capacity + :new.capacite

  WHERE nom = :new.nomCinema;

END;

To guarantee the validity of the cumulation, it would be necessary to create triggers on the events UPDATEand INSERT. A more concise (but more expensive) solution is to systematically recalculate the cumulation: in this case, we can use a trigger that is triggered globally for the request:

CREATE TRIGGER CumulCapaciteGlobal

AFTER UPDATE OR INSERT OR DELETE ON Salle

BEGIN

  UPDATE Cinema C

  SET capacity = (SELECT SUM (capacity)

         FROM Salle S

         WHERE C.nom = S.nomCinema);

END;

The following illustrates the syntax of the CREATE TRIGGER statement:

CREATE TRIGGER [schema_name.]trigger_name

ON table_name

AFTER {[INSERT],[UPDATE],[DELETE]}

[NOT FOR REPLICATION]

AS

{sql_statements}

In this syntax:

The schema_name is the name of the schema to which the new trigger belongs. The schema name is optional.

The trigger_name is the user-defined name for the new trigger.

The table_name is the table to which the trigger applies.

The event is listed in the AFTER clause. The event could be INSERT, UPDATE, or DELETE. A single trigger can fire in response to one or more actions against the table.

The NOT FOR REPLICATION option instructs SQL Server not to fire the trigger when data modification is made as part of a replication process.

The sql_statements is one or more Transact-SQL used to carry out actions once an event occurs.

"Virtual" tables for triggers: INSERTED and DELETED

SQL Server provides two virtual tables that are available specifically for triggers called INSERTED and DELETED tables. SQL Server uses these tables to capture the data of the modified row before and after the event occurs.

The following table shows the content of the INSERTED and DELETED tables before and after each event:

DML event	INSERTED table holds	DELETED table holds
INSERT	rows to be inserted	empty
UPDATE	new rows modified by the update	existing rows modified by the update
DELETE	Empty	rows to be deleted

SQL Server CREATE TRIGGER example

Let's look at an example of creating a new trigger. We will use the production. Products table from the sample database for the demonstration.

production.products
* product_id
product_name
brand_id
category_id
model_year
list_price

1) Create a table for logging the changes

The following statement creates a table named production.product_audits to record information when an INSERT or DELETE event occurs against the production.products table:

```
CREATE TABLE production.product_audits(
    change_id INT IDENTITY PRIMARY KEY,
    product_id INT NOT NULL,
    product_name VARCHAR(255) NOT NULL,
    brand_id INT NOT NULL,
    category_id INT NOT NULL,
    model_year SMALLINT NOT NULL,
    list_price DEC(10,2) NOT NULL,
    updated_at DATETIME NOT NULL,
    operation CHAR(3) NOT NULL,
    CHECK(operation = 'INS' or operation='DEL')
);
```

The production.product_audits table has all the columns from the production.
Products table. In addition, it has a few more columns to record the changes,
e.g., updated_at, operation, and change_id.

2) Creating an after DML trigger

First, to create a new trigger, you specify the name of the trigger and schema to which the
trigger belongs in the CREATE TRIGGER clause:

CREATE TRIGGER production.trg_product_audit

Next, you specify the name of the table, which the trigger will fire when an event occurs,
in the ON clause:

ON production.products

Then, you list the one or more events which will call the trigger in the AFTER clause:

AFTER INSERT, DELETE

The body of the trigger begins with the AS keyword:

AS

BEGIN

After that, inside the body of the trigger, you set the SET NOCOUNT to ON to suppress
the number of rows affected messages from being returned whenever the trigger is fired.

SET NOCOUNT ON;

The trigger will insert a row into the production.product_audits table whenever a row is
inserted into or deleted from the production. Products table. The data for the insert is fed
from the INSERTED and DELETED tables via the UNION ALL operator:

INSERT INTO

  production.product_audits

    (

       product_id,

       product_name,

       brand_id,

       category_id,

       model_year,

       list_price,

       updated_at,

       operation

)

```sql
SELECT
    i.product_id,
    product_name,
    brand_id,
    category_id,
    model_year,
    i.list_price,
    GETDATE(),
    'INS'
FROM
    inserted AS i
UNION ALL
    SELECT
        d.product_id,
        product_name,
        brand_id,
        category_id,
        model_year,
        d.list_price,
        getdate(),
        'DEL'
    FROM
        deleted AS d;
```

The following put all parts together:

```sql
CREATE TRIGGER production.trg_product_audit
ON production.products
AFTER INSERT, DELETE
AS
BEGIN
    SET NOCOUNT ON;
```

```sql
INSERT INTO production.product_audits(
    product_id,
    product_name,
    brand_id,
    category_id,
    model_year,
    list_price,
    updated_at,
    operation
)
SELECT
    i.product_id,
    product_name,
    brand_id,
    category_id,
    model_year,
    i.list_price,
    GETDATE(),
    'INS'
FROM
    inserted i
UNION ALL
SELECT
    d.product_id,
    product_name,
    brand_id,
    category_id,
    model_year,
    d.list_price,
    GETDATE(),
```

'DEL'

FROM

   deleted d;

END

Finally, you execute the whole statement to create the trigger. Once the trigger is created, you can find it under the triggers folder of the table, as shown in the following picture:

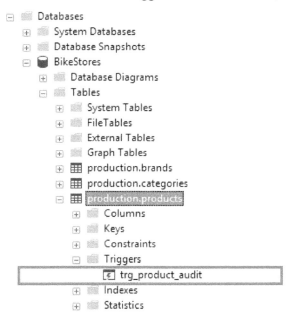

3) Testing the trigger

The following statement inserts a new row into the production.products table:

INSERT INTO production.products(

   product_name,

   brand_id,

   category_id,

   model_year,

   list_price

)

VALUES (

   'Test product',

   1,

   1,

2018,

599

);

Because of the INSERT event, the production.trg_product_audit trigger of production.products table was fired.

Let's examine the contents of the production.product_audits table:

SELECT

*

FROM

production.product_audits;

Here is the output:

change_id	product_id	product_name	brand_id	category_id	model_year	list_price	updated_at	operation
1	322	Test product	1	1	2018	599.00	2018-10-14 15:23:46.837	INS

The following statement deletes a row from the production.products table:

DELETE FROM

production.products

WHERE

product_id = 322;

As expected, the trigger was fired and inserted the deleted row into the production.product_audits table:

SELECT

*

FROM

production.product_audits;

The following picture shows the output:

change_id	product_id	product_name	brand_id	category_id	model_year	list_price	updated_at	operation
1	322	Test product	1	1	2018	599.00	2018-10-14 15:23:46.837	INS
2	322	Test product	1	1	2018	599.00	2018-10-14 15:26:34.050	DEL

In this tutorial, you have learned how to create a trigger in SQL Server to respond to one or more events such as insert and delete.

DIFFERENCE BETWEEN DELETE AND TRUNCATE

DELETE:

DELETE may be a DML (Data Manipulation Language) command and is employed once we specify the row(tuple) that we would like to get rid of or delete from the table or relation. The DELETE command can contain a WHERE clause. If WHERE clause is employed with DELETE command, then it removes or deletes only those rows(tuple) that satisfy the condition; otherwise, by default, it removes all the tuples(rows) from the table.

Syntax of DELETE command:

DELETE FROM TableName

WHERE condition;

TRUNCATE:

TRUNCATE may be a DDL (Data Definition Language) command and is employed to delete all the rows or tuples from a table. Unlike the DELETE command, the TRUNCATE command doesn't contain a WHERE clause. Within the TRUNCATE command, the transaction log for every deleted data page is recorded. Unlike the DELETE command, the TRUNCATE command is fast and that we can't rollback the info after using the TRUNCATE command.

Syntax of TRUNCATE command:-

TRUNCATE TABLE TableName;

Let's see the difference between DELETE and TRUNCATE command:-

S.NO DELETE

1. The DELETE command is employed to delete specified rows(one or more).

2. it's a DML(Data Manipulation Language) command.

3. There could also be a WHERE clause in the DELETE command so as to filter the records.

4. within the DELETE command, a tuple is locked before removing it.

5. we will rollback the info even after using the DELETE command.

6. DELETE command is slower than the TRUNCATE command.

TRUNCATE

1 While this command is employed to delete all the rows from a table.

2 While it's a DDL(Data Definition Language) command.

3 While there might not be WHERE clause in TRUNCATE command.

4 While during this command, the data page is locked before removing the table data.

5 While during this command, we can't rollback.

6 While TRUNCATE command is quicker than DELETE command.

CHAPTER THIRTEEN

HOW TO WRITE STORED PROCEDURES AND FUNCTIONS

SQL Stored Procedures for SQL Server

What is a Stored Procedure?

A stored procedure is a prepared SQL code that you can save, so the code can be reused over and over again.

So, if you have an SQL query that you write over and over again, save it as a stored procedure, and then just call it to execute it.

You can also pass parameters to a stored procedure so that the stored procedure can act based on the parameter value(s) that is passed.

Stored Procedure Syntax

```
CREATE PROCEDURE procedure_name
AS
sql_statement
GO;
```

Execute a Stored Procedure

```
EXEC procedure_name;
```

Demo Database

Below is a selection from the "Customers" table in the Northwind sample database:

CustomerID	CustomerName	ContactName	Address
1	Alfreds Futterkiste	Maria Anders	Obere Str. 57
2	Ana Trujillo Emparedados y helados	Ana Trujillo	Avda. de la Constituciór
3	Antonio Moreno Taquería	Antonio Moreno	Mataderos 2312
4	Around the Horn	Thomas Hardy	120 Hanover Sq.
5	Berglunds snabbköp	Christina Berglund	Berguvsvägen 8

Stored Procedure Example

The following SQL statement creates a stored procedure named "SelectAllCustomers" that selects all records from the "Customers" table:

Example

```
CREATE PROCEDURE SelectAllCustomers
AS
SELECT * FROM Customers
GO;
```

Execute the stored procedure above as follows:

Example

```
EXEC SelectAllCustomers;
```

Stored Procedure With One Parameter

The following SQL statement creates a stored procedure that selects Customers from a particular City from the "Customers" table:

Example

```
CREATE PROCEDURE SelectAllCustomers @City nvarchar(30)
AS
SELECT * FROM Customers WHERE City = @City
GO;
```

Execute the stored procedure above as follows:

Example

```
EXEC SelectAllCustomers @City = 'London';
```

Stored Procedure With Multiple Parameters

Setting up multiple parameters is very easy. Just list each parameter and the data type separated by a comma, as shown below.

The following SQL statement creates a stored procedure that selects Customers from a particular City with a particular PostalCode from the "Customers" table:

Example

```
CREATE PROCEDURE SelectAllCustomers @City nvarchar(30), @PostalCode
nvarchar(10)
AS
SELECT * FROM Customers WHERE City = @City AND PostalCode = @PostalCode
GO;
```

Execute the stored procedure above as follows:

Example

```
EXEC SelectAllCustomers @City = 'London', @PostalCode = 'WA1 1DP';
```

CHAPTER FOURTEEN

HOW TO MAKE DECISIONS WITH IF AND CASE STATEMENTS

SQL CASE

In SQL language, the "CASE… WHEN…" command allows you to use "if / else" type conditions (cf. if / else) similar to a programming language to return an available result between several possibilities. The CASE can be used in any statement or clause, such as SELECT, UPDATE, DELETE, WHERE, ORDER BY, or HAVING.

Syntax

The use of CASE is possible in 2 different ways:

Compare a column to a possible result set

Develop a series of Boolean conditions to determine a result

Compare a column to a result set

Here is the syntax needed to compare a column to a recordset:

BOX a

    WHEN 1 THEN 'one.'

    WHEN 2 THEN 'two.'

    WHEN 3 THEN 'three.'

    ELSE 'other.'

END

In this example, the values contained in the column "a" are compared with 1, 2, or 3. If the condition is true, then the value located after the THEN will be returned.

Note: the ELSE condition is optional and serves as a crumb collector. If the previous conditions are not respected, then the ELSE value will be returned by default.

Develop a series of Boolean conditions to determine a result

It is possible to establish more complex conditions for retrieving one result or another. This is done using the following syntax:

CASE

    WHEN a = b THEN 'A equal to B.'

    WHEN a> b THEN 'A greater than B.'

    ELSE 'A less than B.'

END

In this example, the columns "a," "b," and "c" can contain numerical values. When they are respected, the Boolean conditions allow them to enter one or the other of the conditions.

It is possible to reproduce the first example presented on this page using the following syntax:

CASE

WHEN a = 1 THEN 'one'

WHEN a = 2 THEN 'two.'

WHEN a = 3 THEN 'three.'

ELSE 'other.'

END

Example

To present the CASE in the SQL language, it is possible to imagine a database used by an online sales site. In this database there is a table containing the purchases, this table contains the name of the products, the unit price, the quantity purchased, and a column devoted to a fictitious margin on certain products.

"Purchase" table:

Id	last name	overload	unit price	quantity
1	Product A	1.3	6	3
2	Product B	1.5	8	2
3	Product C	0.75	7	4
4	Product D	1	15	2

Display a message according to a condition

It is possible to carry out a request which will display a personalized message according to the value of the margin. The message will be different depending on whether the margin is equal to 1, greater than one or less than 1. The request can be presented as follows:

SELECT id, name, percentage_ margin, unit_ price, quantity,

   CASE

    WHEN markup_percentage = 1 THEN 'Regular price'

    WHEN margin_percentage> 1 THEN 'Price higher than normal.'

    ELSE 'Lower than the normal price.'

   END

FROM `purchase.`

Result:

Id	last name	overload	unit price	quantity	CASE

Id	last name	overload	unit price	quantity	CASE
1	Product A	1.3	6	3	Price higher than normal
2	Product B	1.5	8	2	Price higher than normal
3	Product C	0.75	7	4	Lower than the normal price
4	Product D	1	15	2	Regular price

This result shows that it is possible to easily display personalized messages under simple conditions.

Display a different unit price according to a condition

With a CASE, it is also possible to use more elaborate queries. Now imagine that we want to multiply the unit price by two if the margin is greater than 1, divide it by two if the margin is less than one, and leave the unit price as it is if the margin is equal to 1. This is possible thanks to the SQL query:

SELECT id, name, percentage_ margin, unit_ price, quantity,

  CASE

    WHEN margin_percentage = 1 THEN price_unit

    WHEN margin_percentage> 1 THEN price_unit * 2

    ELSE unit_price / 2

  END

FROM `purchase.`

Result:

Id	last name	overload	unit price	quantity	CASE
1	Product A	1.3	6	3	12
2	Product B	1.5	8	2	16
3	Product C	0.75	7	4	3.5
4	Product D	1	15	2	15

Compare a field with a given value

Now imagine that the application offers discounts depending on the number of products purchased:

1 product purchased provides a reduction of -5% for the next purchase

2 products purchased allows a reduction of -6% for the next purchase

3 products purchased provides a reduction of -8% for the next purchase

For more products purchased there is a reduction of -10% for the next purchase

To perform such a procedure, it is possible to compare the "quantity" column with the different values specified and display a personalized message depending on the result. This can be done with this SQL query:

SELECT id, name, percentage_ margin, unit_ price, quantity,

  CASE quantity

    WHEN 0 THEN 'Error'

    WHEN 1 THEN '-5% offer for the next purchase.'

    WHEN 2 THEN '-6% offer for the next purchase.'

    WHEN 3 THEN '-8% offer for the next purchase.'

    ELSE '-10% offer for the next purchase.'

  END

 FROM `purchase.`

Result:

Id	last name	overload	unit price	quantity	CASE
1	Product A	1.3	6	3	An offer of -8% for the next purchase
2	Product B	1.5	8	2	An offer of -6% for the next purchase
3	Product C	0.75	7	4	An offer of -10% for the next purchase
4	Product D	1	15	2	An offer of -6% for the next purchase

Tip: the ELSE condition can sometimes be used to handle errors.

UPDATE with CASE

As explained at the beginning, it is also possible to use CASE following the SET command of an UPDATE to update a column with specific data according to a rule. For example, imagine that we want to offer a product for all purchases with an overload of less than one and that we want to withdraw a product for all purchases with an overload of more than 1. You can use the request Following SQL:

```
UPDATE `purchase.`
SET `quantity` = (
  CASE
    WHEN `overload` <1 THEN` quantity` + 1
    WHEN `overload`> 1 THEN` quantity` - 1
    ELSE quantity
  END
)
```

Using the IF Function

If you are using a more modern version of SQL, it is useful to know that SQL Server 2012 introduced the very handy IIF function. IIF is a shorthand method for performing an IF...ELSE/CASE statement and returning one of two values, depending on the evaluation of the result.

Restructuring our above example to use IIF is quite simple.

```
SELECT
  IIF(
    books.title = 'The Hobbit' OR books.primary_author = 'Tolkien',
    'Middle-earth',
    'Earth')
  AS locale,
  books.*
FROM
  books
```

With an IIF function, we largely replace a lot of the syntactical sugar from the CASE statement with a few simple comma-separators to differentiate our arguments

All told, both CASE and IIF get the same job done, but if given a choice, IIF will generally be much simpler to use.

CHAPTER FIFTEEN

HOW TO CONTROL THE FLOW OF PROGRAM WITH WHILE, REPEAT AND LOOP STATEMENTS

The WHILE loop

SQL WHILE loop provides us with the advantage to execute the SQL statement(s) repeatedly until the specified condition result turn out to be false.

In the following sections of this article, we will use more flowcharts in order to explain the notions and examples. For this reason, firstly, we will explain what is a flowchart briefly. The flowchart is a visual geometric symbol that helps to explain algorithms visually. The flowchart is used to simply design and document the algorithms. In the flowchart, each geometric symbol specifies different meanings.

The WHILE loop, a common tool widely used in a large number of programming languages. MySQL is no exception. The syntax is really similar to the others, making it easy to use, but here is a summary. The main keywords you should remember to use a while loop in MySQL are WHILE, DO and END WHILE; When you define a while loop, you can give it a label that can be used by several commands to control the loop. The label comes before the definition of the while loop and after the end of the loop. The following simple example creates a WHILE loop called "iterwhile" that iterates as long as the "iter" variable is less than 9.

Please select

```
DECLARE iter INTEGER DEFAULT 0;

iterwhile: WHILE iter < 9 DO
    SET iter = iter + 1;
END WHILE iterwhile;
```

SQL WHILE loop syntax and example

The syntax of the WHILE loop in SQL looks like as follows:

```
WHILE condition
BEGIN
    {...statements...}
END
```

After these explanations, we will give a very simple example of a WHILE loop in SQL. In the example given below, the WHILE loop example will write a value of the variable ten times, and then the loop will be completed:

```
DECLARE @Counter INT
SET @Counter=1
```

```
WHILE (@Counter <= 10)

BEGIN

    PRINT 'The counter value is = ' +
CONVERT(VARCHAR,@Counter)

    SET @Counter = @Counter + 1

END
```

```
Messages
    The counter value is = 1
    The counter value is = 2
    The counter value is = 3
    The counter value is = 4
    The counter value is = 5
    The counter value is = 6
    The counter value is = 7
    The counter value is = 8
    The counter value is = 9
    The counter value is = 10
```

Now, we will handle the WHILE loop example line by line and examine it with details.

In this part of the code, we declare a variable, and we assign an initializing value to it:

```
DECLARE @Counter
INT

SET @Counter=1
```

This part of the code has a specified condition that until the variable value reaches till 10, the loop continues and executes the PRINT statement. Otherwise, the while condition will not occur, and the loop will end:

```
WHILE ( @Counter <=
10)
```

In this last part of the code, we executed the SQL statement, and then we incremented the value of the variable:

```
BEGIN

    PRINT 'The counter value is = ' +
CONVERT(VARCHAR,@Counter)

    SET @Counter = @Counter + 1

END
```

The following flowchart illustrates this WHILE loop example visually:

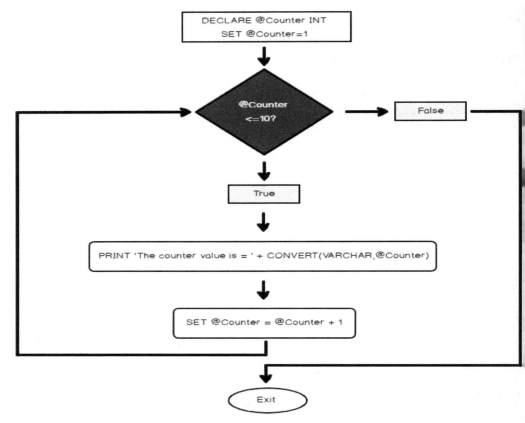

Infinite SQL WHILE loop

In the infinite loop AKA endless loop, the condition result will never be false, so the loop never ends and can work forever. Imagine that we have a WHILE loop, and we don't increment the value of the variable. In this scenario, the loop runs endlessly and never ends. Now, we will realize this scenario with the help of the following example. We need to take account of one thing that we should not forget to cancel the execution of the query manually:

DECLARE @Counter INT

SET @Counter=1

WHILE (@Counter <= 10)

BEGIN

   PRINT 'Somebody stops me!'

END

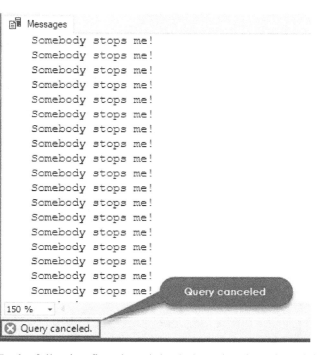

In the following flowchart, it is obvious that the value of the variable never changes; therefore, the loop never ends. The reason for this issue is that the variable is always equal to 1 so the condition returns true for each iteration of the loop:

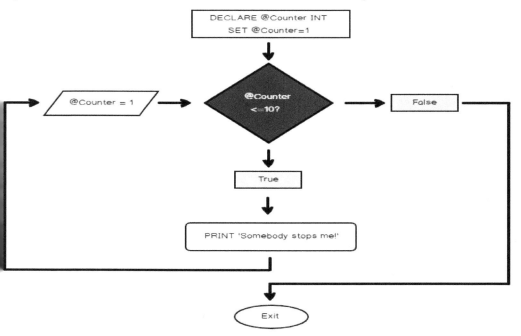

BREAK statement

BREAK statement is used in the SQL WHILE loop in order to exit the current iteration of the loop immediately when certain conditions occur. In the generally IF…ELSE statement is used to check whether the condition has occurred or not. Refer to the SQL IF Statement introduction and overview article for more details about the IF…ELSE statement.

The following example shows the usage of the BREAK statement in the WHILE loop:

DECLARE @Counter INT

SET @Counter=1

WHILE (@Counter <= 10)

BEGIN

  PRINT 'The counter value is = ' +
CONVERT(VARCHAR,@Counter)

  IF @Counter >=7

  BEGIN

  BREAK

  END

  SET @Counter = @Counter + 1

END

```
Messages
    The counter value is = 1
    The counter value is = 2
    The counter value is = 3
    The counter value is = 4
    The counter value is = 5
    The counter value is = 6
    The counter value is = 7
```

In this example, we have checked the value of the variable, and when the value is equal or greater than 7, the code entered the IF…ELSE block and executed the BREAK statement, and so it exited the loop immediately. For this reason, the message shows the values of the variable up to 7. If the condition of the IF…ELSE statement does not meet, and the loop will run until the condition result will be false. The following flowchart explains the working logic of the BREAK statement example as visually:

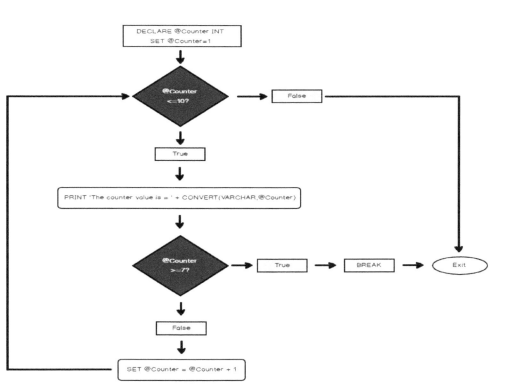

CONTINUE STATEMENT

CONTINUE statement is used in the SQL WHILE loop in order to stop the current iteration of the loop when certain conditions occur, and then it starts a new iteration from the beginning of the loop. Assume that we want to write only even numbers in a WHILE loop. In order to overcome this issue, we can use the CONTINUE statement. In the following example, we will check whether the variable value is odd or even. If the variable value is odd, the code enters the IF…ELSE statement blocks and increment the value of the variable, execute the CONTINUE statement and starts a new iteration:

DECLARE @Counter INT

SET @Counter=1

WHILE (@Counter <= 20)

BEGIN

 IF @Counter % 2 =1

 BEGIN

 SET @Counter = @Counter + 1

 CONTINUE

 END

```
    PRINT 'The counter value is = ' +
CONVERT(VARCHAR,@Counter)

    SET @Counter = @Counter + 1

END
```

🗊 Messages
```
    The counter value is = 2
    The counter value is = 4
    The counter value is = 6
    The counter value is = 8
    The counter value is = 10
    The counter value is = 12
    The counter value is = 14
    The counter value is = 16
    The counter value is = 18
    The counter value is = 20
```

The following flowchart explains the working logic of the CONTINUE statement example as visually:

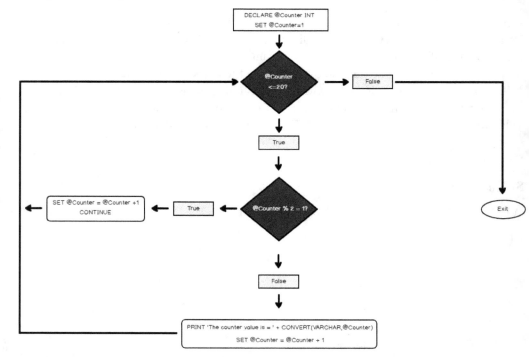

Reading table records through the WHILE loop

In the following example, we will read table data, row by row. Firstly, we will create a sample table:

USE tempdb

GO

DROP TABLE IF EXISTS SampleTable

CREATE TABLE SampleTable

(Id INT, CountryName NVARCHAR (100), ReadStatus TINYINT)

GO

INSERT INTO SampleTable (Id, CountryName, ReadStatus)

Values (1, 'Germany', 0),

    (2, 'France', 0),

    (3, 'Italy', 0),

  (4, 'Netherlands', 0),

   (5, 'Poland', 0)

	Id	CountryName	ReadStatus
1	1	Germany	0
2	2	France	0
3	3	Italy	0
4	4	Netherlands	0
5	5	Poland	0

In this step, we will read all data row by row with the help of the WHILE loop:

 SELECT * FROM SampleTable

USE tempdb

GO

DECLARE @Counter INT, @MaxId INT,

    @CountryName NVARCHAR(100)

SELECT @Counter = min(Id) , @MaxId = max(Id)

FROM SampleTable

WHILE(@Counter IS NOT NULL

   AND @Counter <= @MaxId)

BEGIN

  SELECT @CountryName = CountryName

```
FROM SampleTable WHERE Id = @Counter


PRINT CONVERT(VARCHAR,@Counter) + '. country name is ' +
@CountryName

SET @Counter = @Counter + 1
END
```

```
Messages
    1. country name is Germany
    2. country name is France
    3. country name is Italy
    4. country name is Netherlands
    5. country name is Poland
```

In this example, we read the table rows via the WHILE loop. We can also develop more sophisticated and advanced loops based on our needs.

The LOOP loop

LOOP defines an unconditional loop repeated indefinitely until it is terminated by an EXIT or RETURN instruction. The optional label can be used by EXIT statements in the case of nested loops to define what level of nesting should be completed.

The ultra-simple LOOP command does just that. It loops indefinitely until you ask it to stop with the LEAVE command. Like the WHILE loop, it can be named with a label in its definition so that it can then be targeted by commands to control it. Here is a LOOP command called "iterloop" which does the same thing as the previous WHILE example, but uses an IF command and a LEAVE command to stop.

Please select

DECLARE iter INTEGER DEFAULT 0;

iterloop: LOOP

  IF iter < 9 THEN

    SET iter = iter + 1;

```
    ELSE
        LEAVE iterloop;
    END IF;
END LOOP iterloop;
```

The REPEAT loop

The REPEAT() function repeats a string as many times as specified.
The REPEAT command is essentially a WHILE loop that checks if the conditions
correspond to the end of each iteration, unlike the WHILE, which checks at the start. This
means that when you use the REPEAT loop, it will be executed at least once. Here is
the REPEAT equivalent of WHILE and LOOP was seen previously:

Please select

```
DECLARE iter INTEGER DEFAULT 0;


iterrepeat: REPEAT
    SET iter = iter + 1;
UNTIL iter < 9
END REPEAT iterrepeat;
```

CHAPTER SIXTEEN

WHAT ARE CURSORS AND HOW TO USE THEM?

CURSOR VARIABLES

All cursor accesses in PL / pgSQL are through cursor variables, which are always of the special refcursor data type. One of the ways to make a cursor variable is to easily declare it as a refcursor variable. differently is to use the cursor declaration syntax which is generally:

name [[NO] SCROLL] CURSOR [(arguments)] FOR request;

(FOR are often replaced by IS for compatibility with Oracle ™). If SCROLL is specified, the cursor is going to be ready to reverse; if NO SCROLL is indicated, recoveries within the other way are going to be rejected; if nothing is specified, it depends on the request. Arguments may be a list of knowledge type name pairs that define the names to get replaced by the values of the parameters within the given query. The effective value to substitute for these names is going to be indicated later when the cursor is opened.

Some examples:

DECLARED

curs1 refcursor;

curs2 CURSOR FOR SELECT * FROM tenk1;

curs3 CURSOR (integer key) FOR SELECT * FROM tenk1 WHERE unique1 = cle;

These variables are all three of the refcursor data type, but the primary is often used with any request while the second features a completely specified request which is already linked thereto, and therefore the last is linked to a parameterized request (key are going to be replaced by an integer parameter when opening the cursor). The variable curs1 is claimed to be unbound since it's not linked to a specific request.

Opening cursors

Before a cursor is often wont to retrieve rows, it must be opened (this is that the equivalent action of the SQL DECLARE CURSOR command). PL / pgSQL has three forms for the OPEN statement, two of which use unbound cursor variables and, therefore, the last one a linked cursor variable.

Note

Variables of linked cursors also can be used without opening them explicitly, using the FOR statement described in Section 40.7.4, "Looping through the results of a cursor."

OPEN FOR request

OPEN var_curseur_nonlie [[NO] SCROLL] FOR request;

The cursor variable is opened and receives the required query to execute. The cursor can't be already open, and it must be declared as an unlinked cursor variable (that is, as an easy refcursor variable). The query must be a get or something else that returns rows (like EXPLAIN). The query is treated within the same way because the other SQL commands in PL / pgSQL: the variable names PL / pgSQLare substituted, and therefore, the query plan is cached for possible reuse. When a PL / pgSQL variable is substituted during a cursor type query, the worth that's substituted is that the one it had at the time of OPEN; subsequent changes won't have affected the behavior of the cursor. The choices SCROLL, and NO SCROLL have an equivalent meaning as for a linked cursor.

Example:

OPEN curs1 FOR SELECT * FROM foo WHERE cle = my_cle;

OPEN FOR EXECUTE

OPEN var_curseur_nonlie [[NO] SCROLL] FOR EXECUTE request
  [USING expression [, ...]];

The cursor variable is opened and receives the required query to execute. The cursor can't be already open, and it must be declared as an unlinked cursor variable (that is, as an easy refcursor variable). The query is specified as a string expression within the same way as in an EXECUTE command. As usual, this provides enough flexibility in order that the query plan can change from one execution to a different (see Section 40.10.2, "Plan caching")), and this also means variable substitution isn't done on the command string. Like the EXECUTE command, the parameter values are often inserted into the dynamic command with USING. The choices SCROLL, and NO SCROLL have an equivalent meaning as for a linked cursor.

Example:

OPEN curs1 FOR EXECUTE 'SELECT * FROM' || quote_ident (tabname)

|| 'WHERE col1 = $ 1' USING keyvalue;

In this example, the name of the table is inserted within the query verbatim, and therefore, the use of quote_ident () is suggested so as to protect against SQL injections. The comparison value for col1 is inserted with the USING parameter and thus doesn't get to be protected.

Opening a linked cursor

OPEN var_curseur_lié [([argument_name : =] argument_value [, ...])];

This form of OPEN is employed to open a cursor variable to which the query is linked at the time of declaration. The cursor can't be already open. An inventory of argument expressions should appear if and as long as the cursor has been declared to simply accept arguments. These values are going to be replaced within the query.

The query plan for a linked cursor is usually considered cacheable; there's no equivalent of the EXECUTE command during this case. Note that SCROLL and NO SCROLL can't be laid out in OPEN because the cursor behavior was already determined.

Argument values are often passed using either a positional representation system or named notation. Within the first, all the arguments are listed so as. Within the second, each argument's name is indicated using: = to separate it from the argument expression. Almost like the call, described in Section 4.3, "Calling functions," it's also allowed to combine notation in position and named notation.

Here are some examples (they use the cursor declaration examples above):

OPEN curs2;

OPEN curs3 (42);

OPEN curs3 (key: = 42);

Since variable substitution is completed on the request of a linked cursor, there are actually two ways of passing values to the cursor: either with a particular argument for OPEN or by implicitly referencing a PL / pgSQL variable within the request. However, only the variables declared before the linked cursor is said are going to be substituted for it. Altogether cases, the worth passed is decided at the time of the execution of the OPEN command. For instance, differently to urge an equivalent effect because the curs3 example above is as follows:

DECLARED

 key integer;

 curs4 CURSOR FOR SELECT * FROM tenk1 WHERE unique1 = key;

BEGIN

 key: = 42;

 OPEN curs4;

Using cursors

Once a cursor has been opened, it is often manipulated using the instructions described below.

These manipulations don't get to happen within the same function as that which opened the cursor. You'll return a refcursor value from a function and let the caller operate the cursor (from an indoor point of view, a refcursor value is just the character string of the name of a portal containing the active request for the cursor. This name is often passed to others, assigned to other refcursor variables than on, without disturbing the portal).

All portals are implicitly closed at the top of the transaction. Are often "> this is often why a refcursor value can be wont to reference an open cursor only until the top of the transaction.

FETCH

FETCH [direction {FROM | IN] target INTO cursor;

FETCH retrieves subsequent line from a cursor and places it during a target, which may be a line variable, a record variable, or an inventory of straightforward variables separated by commas, as during a SELECT INTO. If there's no next row, the target is about to NULL. Like SELECT INTO, the special variable FOUND is often read to ascertain if a row has been retrieved.

The direction clause is often one among the subsequent variants authorized for the SQL FETCH (7) command, except those which may retrieve quite one line; namely, it is often NEXT, PRIOR, FIRST, LAST, ABSOLUTE number, RELATIVE number, FORWARD or BACKWARD. Omitting direction is the same as specifying NEXT. Within the syntax using count, the variable count is often any expression returning an integer (unlike the FETCH command, which only allows an integer constant). Direction values that require getting into the other direction may fail unless the cursor has been declared or opened with the SCROLL option.

The cursor must be the name of a refcursor variable that references an open cursor portal.

Examples:

FETCH curs1 INTO rowvar;

FETCH curs2 INTO foo, bar, baz;

FETCH LAST FROM curs3 INTO x, y;

RELATIVE FETCH -2 FROM curs4 INTO x;

MOVE

MOVE [direction {FROM | IN}] cursor;

 MOVE reposition a cursor without retrieving data. MOVE works exactly just like the FETCH command except that it only repositions the cursor and thus doesn't return the lines of the displacement. Like SELECT INTO, the special variable FOUND is often read to see if there have been indeed the lines like the displacement.

Examples:

MOVE curs1;

MOVE LAST FROM curs3;

MOVE RELATIVE -2 FROM curs4;

MOVE FORWARD 2 FROM curs4;

UPDATE / DELETE WHERE CURRENT OF

UPDATE table SET ... WHERE CURRENT OF cursor;

DELETE FROM table WHERE CURRENT OF cursor;

When a cursor is positioned on a row of a table, this row is often updated or deleted using the cursor, which identifies the row. There are restrictions on what the cursor request are often (in particular, no grouping), and it's best to use FOR UPDATE within the cursor. For further information, see the DECLARE reference page (7).

An example:

UPDATE foo SET valdonnee = mavaleur WHERE CURRENT OF curs1;

CLOSE

CLOSE cursor;

CLOSE closes the portal underlying an open cursor. This will be wont to free resources before the top of the transaction or to free the cursor variable to be ready to reopen it.

Example:

CLOSE curs1;

RETURNING CURSORS

Functions PL / pgSQL can return cursors to the caller. This is often useful for returning multiple rows or columns, especially with very large result sets. To try to do this, the function opens the cursor and returns the cursor name to the caller (or simply opens the cursor employing a portal name specified by or otherwise known to the caller). The caller can then retrieve the lines from the cursor. The cursor is often closed by the caller, or it'll be closed automatically at the top of the transaction.

The portal name used for a cursor is often specified by the developer or is often generated automatically. To specify a portal name, simply assign a string to the variable refcursor before opening it. The worth of the variable refcursor is going to be employed by OPEN because of the name of the underlying portal. However, if the variable refcursor is NULL OPEN automatically generates a reputation that doesn't conflict with any existing portal and assigns it to the variable refcursor.

Note

A cursor variable with limits is initialized with the value of the string representing its name so that the portal name is identical to the name of the cursor variable unless the developer overloads it by assignment before opening the cursor. But, a cursor variable without limit will have by default the value NULL, from which it receives a unique name generated automatically unless it is overloaded.

The following example shows one way to provide a cursor name to the caller:

CREATE TABLE test (col text);

INSERT INTO test VALUES ('123');

CREATE FUNCTION reference_function (refcursor) RETURNS refcursor AS $$

BEGIN

   OPEN $ 1 FOR SELECT col FROM test;

   RETURN $ 1;

END;

$$ LANGUAGE plpgsql;

BEGIN;

SELECT reference_function ('function_cursor');

FETCH ALL IN function_cursor;

COMMIT;

The following example uses automatic generation of the cursor name:

CREATE FUNCTION reference_function2 () RETURNS refcursor AS $$

DECLARED

   ref refcursor;

```
BEGIN
    OPEN ref FOR SELECT col FROM test;
    RETURN ref;
END;
$$ LANGUAGE plpgsql;
```

- You must be in a transaction to use the cursors.

```
BEGIN;
SELECT reference_function2 ();
```

```
   reference_function2
--------------------------
 <unnamed cursor 1>
(1 row)
```

```
FETCH ALL IN "<unnamed cursor 1>";
COMMIT;
```

The following example shows one way to return multiple cursors to a single function:

```
CREATE FUNCTION my_function (refcursor, refcursor) RETURNS SETOF refcursor
AS $$
BEGIN
    OPEN $ 1 FOR SELECT * FROM table_1;
    RETURN NEXT $ 1;
    OPEN $ 2 FOR SELECT * FROM table_2;
    RETURN NEXT $ 2;
END;
$$ LANGUAGE plpgsql;
```

- must be in a transaction to use the cursors.

```
BEGIN;
```

SELECT * FROM my_function ('a', 'b');

FETCH ALL FROM a;

FETCH ALL FROM b;

COMMIT;

Looping through cursor results

It is a variant of the FOR statement which allows iteration on the lines returned by a cursor. The syntax is:

[<< label >>]

FOR var_record IN var_curseur_lié [([argument_name : =] argument_value [, ...])]
LOOP

    instructions

END LOOP [label];

The cursor variable must have been linked to a query when it was declared, and it cannot be already open. The FOR statement automatically opens the cursor, and it closes the cursor at the end of the loop. A list of argument value expressions should appear if and only if the cursor has been declared to take arguments. These values will be substituted in the request, in the same way as during an OPEN

The variable var_record is automatically defined with the record type and exists only in the loop (any existing definition of a variable name is ignored in the loop). Each line returned by the cursor is successively assigned to the record variable, and the body of the loop is executed.